# Hernán Cortés

HEATHER LEHR WAGNER

# GREAT EXPLORERS

# Hernán Cortés

HEATHER LEHR WAGNER

CHELSEA HOUSE
PUBLISHERS
An imprint of Infobase Publishing

**GREAT EXPLORERS: HERNÁN CORTÉS**

Chelsea House
An imprint of Infobase Publishing
132 West 31st Street
New York NY 10001

**Library of Congress Cataloging-in-Publication Data**
Wagner, Heather Lehr.
  Hernán Cortés / Heather Lehr Wagner.
    p. cm. — (Great explorers)
  Includes bibliographical references and index.
  ISBN 978-1-60413-424-7 (hardcover)
  1. Cortés, Hernán, 1485-1547—Juvenile literature. 2. Mexico—History—Conquest, 1519—1540—Juvenile literature. 3. Mexico—Discovery and exploration—Spanish—Juvenile literature. 4. Explorers—Mexico—Biography—Juvenile literature. 5. Explorers—Spain—Biography—Juvenile literature. 6. Conquerors—Mexico—Biography—Juvenile literature. I. Title. II. Series.
  F1230.C835W34 2009
  972'.02092—dc22
  [B]                        2009014165

Series design by Lina Farinella
Cover design by Keith Trego

Printed in the United States of America

Bang EJB 10 9 8 7 6 5 4 3 2 1

This book is printed on acid-free paper.

All links and Web addresses were checked and verified to be correct at the time of publication. Because of the dynamic nature of the Web, some addresses and links may have changed since publication and may no longer be valid.

# CONTENTS

# The Quest Begins

FOR 15 YEARS, HERNÁN CORTÉS HAD ENJOYED A COMFORTABLE life in the West Indies, Spain's most prized colonies (known today as "the Caribbean Islands"). He had left his home in Medellín, Spain, at the age of 19, determined to follow the tales of incredible riches in the New World. He sailed on board a merchant ship to Santo Domingo, the capital of Hispaniola (the island now known as Haiti), where Columbus had landed less than 10 years earlier.

The West Indies had changed rapidly since Columbus first explored them, and Santo Domingo was a busy port city by the time Cortés reached it in 1504. Still much was unknown about the area of the Caribbean and the Gulf of Mexico. Explorations were launched from Hispaniola seeking gold as well as new lands to claim in the name of the Spanish ruler.

At first Cortés led a relatively quiet life in his new home. He worked in local politics, obtained some land, built a home, and raised crops. Then, in 1509, Don Diego Columbus, the son

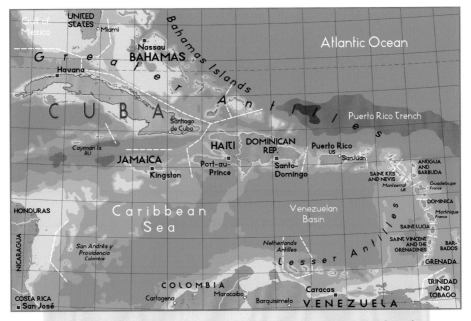

After Christopher Columbus's voyages to the Americas, Spanish and Portuguese explorers became rivals for the wealth and land still undiscovered in Central and South America. Later, they began to enslave the native population and establish profitable colonies.

of the legendary explorer, arrived in Santo Domingo. He had been appointed governor of the Indies, and he determined to more thoroughly explore the new lands he was supposed to govern. First, he explored Puerto Rico. Next, in 1511, he turned his sights to Cuba. At the time, knowledge of Cuba was so sketchy that it was not thought to be an island at all, but instead part of some larger mainland.

The Cuba expedition was headed by Diego Velázquez, who led a force of some 300 men to conquer the island. Cortés was one of them. He was 26 years old, and was then working as clerk to the treasurer, with responsibility for ensuring that an adequate portion of any riches discovered in the New World was forwarded to the Spanish king. The conquest was quickly accomplished. Velázquez was appointed lieutenant-governor of Cuba, and in gratitude for Cortés's assistance in the mission he was given substantial property in the new colony.

Cortés contentedly settled in what would become the new colony's capital, Santiago. There he steadily began accumulating both influence and wealth. He earned the trust of Velázquez. As Velázquez became governor of Cuba, Cortés also became more politically powerful, serving as notary, as Velázquez's secretary-treasurer, and finally as *alcalde*, or mayor, of Santiago.

In Cuba, Cortés witnessed the launch of several expeditions whose goal was to explore the Yucatán (in the area we know today as Mexico), across the Caribbean Sea from Cuba's western coast. These expeditions returned with gold, with tales of Indian towns and large stone temples, and of battles fought against fierce warriors. They also returned with evidence that, at last, the mainland and the vast supply of gold that had long been sought had been found.

Velázquez quickly wanted to ensure that he would be appointed governor of this vast new territory. He needed someone he could trust, someone wealthy enough to finance the majority of the expedition on his own, and someone who had experience in conquering new territory. The perfect candidate was Hernán Cortés.

## Planning the Mission

Cortés was eager to accept the mission, so eager that he was willing to risk his entire fortune on it. He mortgaged his estate to raise the sum needed to pay for the ships and supplies necessary for the journey. While Velázquez wanted the new land colonized as part of the greater Cuba territory he was governing, the official contract he signed with Cortés appointing him captain-general of the mission set out other goals. The agreement the two men signed on October 23, 1518, stated that the mission was to focus on exploration and discovery, converting the people they might meet to the Christian faith and persuading them to accept Spanish rule.

Cortés understood something about pageantry, and while his ships were being prepared for the voyage he had two special flags created. According to Hammond Innes in *The Conquistadors*, these flags were embroidered with gold thread and bore the royal coat of arms and a cross on each side, with the words "Brothers and Comrades, let us follow the sign of the Holy Cross in true faith, for under this sign we shall conquer." He recruited men to join him, promising them a portion of the gold and silver and whatever treasure was found, as well as what were then known as *encomiendas*—the legal rights to a certain amount of native workers to provide slave labor. The stories of the wealth to be found in this new territory spread throughout Cuba, and many men willingly joined the expedition.

Cortés had studied the prior expeditions that had set out from the West Indies to explore new territories and understood what was needed for a successful mission. He used the money from his mortgaged estate to buy plentiful supplies, weapons, and items that could be traded with the people they would meet. Soon Cortés was seen walking about the streets of Santiago with an armed group of followers, according to Innes, "wearing a plume of feathers with a medallion and a chain of gold and a velvet cloak trimmed with gold."

By this time he already had six ships ready for the journey and a group of about 300 men who had signed up to join him. He had also made more than a few enemies, some of them jealous of his success, others who hoped to discredit him and persuade Velázquez to let them lead the expedition instead.

The sight of so many ships, weapons, and armed followers operating under the direction of one of his citizens no doubt was worrisome to Velázquez. Gradually he became convinced that perhaps it might not have been wise to give away so much control over the mission. Word of this change of heart quickly reached Cortés, who decided that his expedition had better set off—immediately. He quickly sent a team of men out to buy all of the meat in the town and then ordered his 300 men to set sail. The ships hastily weighed anchor on the morning of November 18, 1518. Cortés himself was in a boat full of his most trusted men, all of them heavily armed, as they sailed out of harbor, just ahead of the force Velázquez had sent to arrest him.

## Final Preparations

Cortés's hasty departure had saved him from arrest, but he still needed to complete his preparations for the journey. He ordered his fleet to sail to Trinidad, where he spent time with Juan de Grijalva, who had made an earlier journey to the Yucatán. Cortés was able to persuade some of those who had traveled with Grijalva to join his crew. He also gained several more ships while in Trinidad and yet again successfully avoided Velázquez's efforts to arrest him, this time by marching about surrounded by heavily armed guards who intimidated the local officials.

Finally, the preparations were complete. The force Cortés had assembled to begin his conquest of this new territory was impressive. His fleet included 11 ships; the largest was the 100-ton *Santa María de la Concepción*, on which Cortés sailed. There were also three ships, weighing 70 to 80 tons, and several smaller boats. The larger ships also carried boats that could be lowered into the water to transport small crews to shore when land was reached.

The ships all carried supplies needed to last for a lengthy voyage, in this case the kind of food that was plentiful in Trinidad. There was salt pork—similar to bacon but fattier

The stories of Columbus and other explorers inspired Cortés (*above*) to follow a path as a pioneer and colonizer. Cortés became a politician in Cuba and the leader of an expedition to explore and colonize the interior of the Yucatán Peninsula for Spain.

and not smoked—as well as corn, yucca (a root vegetable), and chilies.

Having heard stories of the fierce fighters previous expeditions to the region had encountered, Cortés made sure that his fleet was well stocked with ammunition and gunpowder, as well as cannons, matchlocks (a forerunner of the rifle), crossbows, and arrows.

Cortés also paid careful attention to the crew with whom he would be sailing. They numbered more than 500 by the time his preparations were complete. Buddy Levy in *Conquistador* notes that the crew included pikemen (men skilled in handling the pike, or sharply pointed spike), swordsmen, lancers (a lance was a long spear used by soldiers mounted on horseback when charging), artillerymen, cavalrymen (and the horses they would ride), and blacksmiths (to repair the weapons and care for the horses' shoes). Cortés had also brought some 200 native Cubans—men to perform manual labor and women to cook and mend the clothing.

It was an impressive fighting force that finally set sail on February 10, 1519. Bernal Díaz, who was one of the soldiers sailing with Cortés, described his leader in his account of the journey, *The Conquest of New Spain*, as "a good horseman and skillful with all weapons on foot or on horseback. . . . In everything, in his presence as well as in his talk and conversation, in his table and his dress, in everything he showed signs of being a great lord." The men who had signed up for the journey were eager to explore this new land, to find gold and riches. They were also fiercely loyal. "We would all have laid down our lives for Cortés," Díaz wrote in his memoir.

The expedition that set out in 1519 would discover the land, and the gold, they sought. But their arrival on the shores of the country we know today as Mexico would bring almost unimaginable suffering to the people they encountered. Cortés would succeed in his ambitions, not only claiming a vast new land for Spain but also defeating the powerful Aztec ruler, Montezuma, and conquering his 15 million subjects. The voyage that began that fateful day in 1519 would mark not only the beginning of the discovery of the Aztec nation, but also the beginning of its destruction.

# The Spanish Empire

HERNÁN (ALSO KNOWN AS HERNANDO) CORTÉS WAS BORN in Medellín, in Spain's Castile region, in 1485. His father was Martín Cortés, a minor nobleman who, despite his title, was relatively poor. Martín Cortés was an infantryman, and had fought in several of the wars that marked life in Spain during the second half of the fifteenth century. By the time his son was born, Martín was managing a small farm (with a modest vineyard and wheat fields) while living in a house in the main square of Medellín.

Hernán Cortés's mother, Doña Catalina Pizarro Altimirano, was the daughter of a former soldier; her father (Cortés's grandfather) was active in the politics of Medellín and served as a magistrate. She was a distant relative of the man who would become the conqueror of Peru, Francisco Pizarro.

At the time of Cortés's birth, Medellín was a city of some 2,500 people, located at a strategic point on the main road between Guadalupe and Seville. The city was dominated by a

In order to cement their power and respond to the religious fervor sweeping through their country, Queen Isabella and King Ferdinand issued an edict expelling all of the Jewish citizens from Spain in 1492 (*depicted above*). An estimated 200,000 people (some scholars say up to 800,000) were exiled and the most distinguished and largest Jewish settlement in Europe ended. The expulsion was so tragic that 1492 has become a date almost as important in Jewish history as it is in American history.

large castle (the property of the count of Medellín), and at the time of Cortés's birth contained Christian, Muslim, and Jewish inhabitants. When he was seven years old, Cortés witnessed a dramatic change in the population of his hometown. Queen Isabella and King Ferdinand of Spain signed a decree in 1492 expelling all Jews from their lands. The move was a response to the religious fervor sweeping through much of Spain and the increasing power of the Catholic Church. The Jewish inhabitants of Medellín were forced to leave their homes; many of them relocated to Portugal (from where they would be forced out a few years later).

This was the earliest impact that Ferdinand and Isabella had on the life of Hernán Cortés. Their reign marked a dramatic shift in daily life in Spain as it moved from a quarreling cluster of kingdoms to a modern, powerful nation that would colonize a new world.

## Unifying a Kingdom

The Spain that existed at the time of Cortés's birth and childhood was a relatively new creation, its peace the result of decades of civil war. In the eighth century, much of the peninsula occupied today by Spain and Portugal fell to invaders from North Africa who brought with them Islam and set up a Muslim system of rule (or *caliphate*) based in Córdoba. It would be some 700 years and numerous wars before most of Spain was reconquered; Andalusia (known then as al-Andalus) in the south was the last to fall.

The reconquest of Spain was not simply a story of religious wars between Christian and Muslim forces. It was a far more complex story, with new kingdoms established in the regions seized from Muslim control, with northern kingdoms facing off against those in the south, and with no clear national identity to mark one territory from the other. These divisions would continue to mark Spain even at the time of Cortés's birth.

The marriage of Ferdinand and Isabella is of particular significance in this transformation of Spain from a peninsula of warring states to a powerful kingdom. They were married in a small ceremony on October 19, 1469, some 16 years before Cortés was born. At the time, they were each heirs to two of the most powerful states in Spain—the 17-year-old Ferdinand was heir to the throne of Aragon, and Isabella, at 18, was an heiress to the throne of Castile. The two had traveled to the place where they would be married separately, in disguise, and accompanied only by their most trusted aides. The reason for the secrecy was that there were many powerful people eager to prevent this marriage—and the union of two kingdoms it would produce—from taking place. Within Castile, Isabella's right to succeed to the throne was being challenged by powerful noblemen who had no wish to see a strong monarch installed to rule over them. King Louis XI of France was one who recognized that two powerful kingdoms unified in neighboring Spain might ultimately challenge France's territory.

When Ferdinand's father, Juan II of Aragon, died in 1479, Ferdinand became king and the young king and queen began the process of unifying their kingdoms. In an effort to stabilize their lands, Isabella and Ferdinand organized local militia. They traveled throughout their land, creating alliances and often settling disputes personally. Henry Kamen in *Empire: How Spain Became a World Power* quoted an admiral of Castile, who said of the pair, "They were rulers of our realm, of our speech, born and bred among us. They knew everybody, gave honors to those who merited them, travelled through their realms, were known by great and small alike, and could be reached by all."

Noblemen who had been trained in battle for territory within Spain were instead encouraged to plan campaigns of conquest in new lands, rather than fighting each other. Cortés's father, Martín, had been a cavalryman in one of the civil wars; Cortés would lead cavalry in battle against a distant empire.

The year 1492 marked a decisive turning point in the reign of Ferdinand and Isabella. In January, their army marched into Granada, a city in southern Spain under Muslim rule, and claimed it for their kingdom of Castile. Next, the Jewish population was forced out of all of the lands over which they ruled. In mid-April, a sailor from Genoa in Italy, Christopher Columbus, received Isabella's support for his plan to explore the seas that bordered Spain's western shore and discover a new route to Asia. He returned one year later with exciting reports of what he claimed was a new route to the Orient.

Gradually, King Ferdinand would begin to describe the expulsion of Jews and the effort to control Granada and seize more of the Andalusian territory around it as part of a religious crusade. Soldiers from other parts of Europe arrived to join this "holy war."

This war effectively unified the various parts of Spain. In the territories where Islam had been practiced, inhabitants were forced to convert to Christianity.

Cortés would be greatly influenced by these events of 1492. The adventures of Columbus would inspire some, including Cortés, to follow the path he had pioneered across the sea. The conquest of Granada would give rise to a generation of "conquistadors" seeking new lands to conquer and new people to convert to Christianity.

## The Influence of Columbus

Columbus believed that he had discovered a new route to Asia, but it was the gold he brought back with him that helped convince Ferdinand and Isabella to fund additional expeditions. In 1493 Columbus led a far larger convoy of some 17 ships and 1,200 men, whose mission was to settle Hispaniola (the island Columbus had discovered in the Caribbean) and explore the additional islands in the region—and to bring back more gold. Columbus returned in 1496, this time accompanied by several of Hispaniola's residents, whom Columbus presented to the monarchs as slaves.

Columbus painted a picture of a peaceful land, rich in gold and people who could be forced into slavery, but lacking the spices he had hoped to find in this route to the Orient. Columbus wrote in his journal (as quoted in Henry Kamen's *Empire*) that the people of Hispaniola were "without skill at arms, a thousand running away from three [Spaniards], and thus they

Columbus's expeditions were funded by the Spanish king and queen, who had hopes of adding to their empire. Columbus was unable to find the gold that his investors desired, so he went from island to island filling his ships with native captives. This painting shows the return of Columbus from one of his voyages, with the men, women, and children he had captured to be used as slaves.

are good to be ordered about, to be made to work, plant and do whatever is wanted, to build towns and be taught to go clothed and accept our customs."

Columbus made two additional trips to the region, exploring Trinidad and reaching the mainland of South America in 1489–1500 and exploring the coast of Honduras in 1502–1504, before he died in 1506. He had traveled sufficiently through the territory to realize that it was not a quick route to Asia, as he had initially hoped, although the region would carry the misleading name "the West Indies" long after this fact was clear. From the accounts of those who sailed with Columbus, it was clear that the journey was challenging and life on the islands could be difficult. Still, the gold inspired a few seeking their fortunes to follow in Columbus's footsteps.

Among the men accompanying Columbus on his second journey to the New World were several men from the area where Cortés lived, including at least one—Luis Hernández Portocarrero—from his hometown of Medellín. The stories and rumors of what had been discovered would have spread through Medellín and fed the imagination of the young boy.

Few specific details are known of Cortés's childhood. He was an only child, and a sick one. Cortés credited the prayers of a nurse who cared for him when he was an infant—prayers to Saint Peter—for saving his life when his parents believed he would not survive, and throughout his life he would cite the saint he called "San Pedro" as a leading force in his success.

Sickness continued to plague Cortés as a young boy. Because of his physical frailness, his parents decided that a life in the military would not be possible. At first they explored the possibility of his becoming a page (an attendant to a member of the noble family living at the castle at Medellín—this was the first step toward becoming a knight in medieval society). When they failed to find him a place there, they turned to the church. Cortés became an acolyte (an assistant to the priests), his parents perhaps believing that he would ultimately enter the priesthood.

The time spent performing minor duties in the church did shape Cortés. In his efforts to conquer Mexico he would use rituals and dramatic preaching to help convert the people he encountered.

When he was 12 years old, Cortés left Medellín, although he would not forget his ties to the city. When he had made a fortune in the New World, he sent gifts to the count of Medellín, many of his closest friends and advisers were from the Extremadura region, and he named a town in Mexico after his hometown.

Cortés went to live with his aunt in Salamanca, the city where his father had been born. By this time he was preparing for a career in government, as a civil servant, and so he studied Latin, law, and grammar. He spent five years there, gradually becoming convinced that he was not destined for a career in the government but instead for something more adventurous, either traveling to the Indies like Columbus, or going to fight as part of the Spanish force fighting in Italy. Several of his relatives, including his uncle, had chosen the latter path.

Cortés returned to Medellín in 1501. He was 17 years old, and his parents were not pleased when they learned of his plans. They had hoped he would follow in his grandfather's footsteps and choose a career as a civil servant. It was a safe and profitable way to make a living.

Instead Cortés chose to travel to the Indies. The stories of gold had inspired him, and he liked the idea of setting out across the waters to a new land. A cousin was making plans for a journey in 1502 under the command of Nicolás de Ovando, who was also a distant relative of the Cortés family. Cortés decided to join him, and travelled to Seville, where the plans for the expedition were being finalized.

Ovando planned to take 32 ships with him, sailing to Hispaniola with pigs, chickens, horses, and cows. The city of Seville was, in addition to being the largest city in Spain at the time, also an important port from which many Spanish sea journeys were launched. There were merchants from Genoa there, sailors from Italy, printers from Germany, slaves from Africa. The king and queen spent time in Seville that year, and the city was marked by cathedrals (including an enormous one under construction), large palaces, and paved streets. The waters were full of ships, preparing for voyages, including Ovando's, and Cortés would have been surrounded by stories of adventures planned and those already fulfilled.

Cortés's own adventure abruptly ended in an embarrassing gesture of romance. While waiting for his ship to be ready to sail, Cortés had met a girl. One night, while trying to climb into (or perhaps out of) her window, Cortés fell. His injury was serious enough that he could not join the expedition, and as he recovered he caught a strain of malaria that further weakened him.

By the time Cortés had recovered, Ovando's ships had sailed, and there were no expeditions leaving for the Indies. He reconsidered his plans and decided that he might travel to Italy to join the Spanish forces there after all.

He traveled to Valencia, Spain's main port city and the point from which he could take a ship to Naples in nearby Italy. But then he hesitated. Rather than boarding a ship immediately, he explored the city and once more was captured by the idea of sea travel. After exploring the city, he returned to Seville where, finally, in the summer of 1504, he paid for his passage aboard the *Trinidad*. He was 19 years old and, at last, he was bound for Hispaniola.

# A New World

HERNÁN CORTÉS WAS 19 YEARS OLD WHEN HE FIRST SAW THE New World where he planned to make his fortune. The *Trinidad* on which he sailed across the Atlantic Ocean was part of a fleet of five ships bound for Santo Domingo, the capital of Hispaniola. When Cortés reached Hispaniola, its governor was Nicolás de Ovando, the man with whom Cortés had initially hoped to sail to the New World. One of Ovando's secretaries was a man named Medina, who also was a friend of Cortés. Medina invited Cortés to stay with him while he settled into life there.

Medina quickly began to give Cortés advice about life in Hispaniola. He told him to register as a citizen, a legal step that would entitle him to a *caballería*—a building plot and land to farm. This was not exactly the quick path to riches Cortés had expected to find in the New World, and the streets paved with gold that had been rumored of in Spain were lacking in the bustling capital of Santo Domingo. Later, Cortés met with Governor Ovando himself, who gave the young man similar advice about registering as a citizen and also gave him a *repartimiento* (supervision over a number of indigenous workers) of Indians to be his servants.

Cortés apparently settled into life as a modest landowner. Governor Ovando appointed him notary to the town council of Azúa, a town Ovando had recently founded, which consisted of a church, a fortress, and one or two houses. Over the next five years, Cortés gradually established himself as a civil servant and formed connections that would prove useful in the future.

Hispaniola had become a launching point for several expeditions to explore the surrounding islands and seek the mainland whose geography was still uncertain. Cortés soon learned of one that was being organized by Diego de Nicuesa and Alonso de Hojeda, two Spaniards who, in 1509, decided to explore the Atlantic Coast of what we know today as Colombia and Panama, setting up a base in Jamaica, an area previously discovered during one of Columbus's expeditions.

Cortés decided to join the expedition and was only prevented from sailing with it at the last moment, by a painful abscess on his right leg behind the knee. It was a fortunate development, as the Nicuesa-Hojeda expedition would prove disastrous. More than a thousand of those who participated lost their lives during battles with the inhabitants of the territories, or from hunger and extreme dehydration, as well as other illnesses. Francisco Pizarro, who later would conquer Peru, was one of the lucky ones who participated in the expedition and survived.

## Exploring Cuba

Cortés gradually recovered, and when in 1511 a force was dispatched from Hispaniola to conquer Cuba, Cortés was one of the 300 men who made up the force. The expedition had been ordered by Diego Columbus, the son of the famed explorer, and it was Diego Columbus who had been appointed governor

Initially, Diego Velázquez (*right*) supported Cortés's expedition to Mexico, but then changed his mind after their relationship became strained. Ignoring Velázquez's order to cease the voyage, Cortés (*left*) went anyway in an open act of mutiny. Throughout Cortés's time in Mexico, Velázquez continued to oppose Cortés.

of the Indies in 1509. Diego Columbus had come to Santo Domingo and then ordered expeditions to complete his father's work. The first went to the island of Puerto Rico; then came Cuba.

By the time Columbus ordered the expedition to Cuba, it was known that Cuba was an island, not—as had originally been supposed—part of a larger mainland. But the island had not been explored. The expedition was under the command of Diego Velázquez.

Cortés was 26 years old. He had been appointed clerk to the treasurer, a job that gave him the responsibility for ensuring that the king received one-fifth of any wealth from the New World.

Cuba was quickly conquered, and Velázquez was appointed its lieutenant-governor, with Cortés serving as his secretary. A large number of the native Cubans living on the island were given as servants to two men: Cortés and Juan Juárez, a Spaniard from Granada who had arrived in Santo Domingo in 1509 and then brought to Cuba his mother and three sisters. The sisters had come hoping to meet wealthy husbands, and because they were attractive and there were very few Spanish women in the islands, they quickly became very popular.

Juárez had received the generous grant of servants from Velázquez because the lieutenant-governor had fallen in love with one of his sisters. Cortés began to spend time with one of the other sisters, Catalina. By now Cortés had become a prosperous man. In addition to his important position as secretary to Velázquez, he owned mines, cattle, sheep, and a comfortable home in the newly established town of Santiago de Baracoa. He also had a reputation for romancing women, and while he enjoyed spending time with Catalina, he had no plans to marry her.

The disappointed Catalina set the stage for a more serious plot against Cortés, for by now because of his success he had also made some enemies, who were jealous of his wealth, the slaves he had been given, and his prominent position in the community. They took advantage of Velázquez's relationship with one of the Juárez sisters to incite his anger against Cortés for refusing to marry another of the sisters.

According to Cortés's secretary, Francisco López de Gómara, who wrote a biography of Cortés in 1552, Cortés was accused before Velázquez of "many wicked deeds in the affairs that had been entrusted to him; moreover [they said] that he had some strange and secret dealings with several people." Velázquez responded by first publicly scolding Cortés and then arresting him and putting him in prison.

Cortés feared the results of a trial, and so broke the padlock on his cell and escaped through the prison window. He then hurried to the local church, where he could safely find sanctuary.

Velázquez was furious at Cortés for defying his orders, and ordered his capture. Cortés remained safe for several days until, in a careless moment (some reports suggest that Catalina was used as a lure) he was recaptured, put in shackles, and placed onboard a ship. Cortés feared that he might be sent back to Santo Domingo or, worse, to Spain, and determined to escape. He was fortunate that many felt that Velázquez was letting his relationship with the Juárez family influence his actions, and a friendly servant boy onboard the ship agreed to exchange clothes with Cortés. Cortés slipped out of the shackles, put on the servant's clothes, and slipped over the side of the prison vessel in a small boat used to transport people to and from shore.

There was only one other boat in the harbor. Cortés rowed quietly up to it and cut loose the ropes that tied it to the larger vessel, so that if he were spotted, no one would be able to chase him. Unfortunately, the Macaniagua River had a very strong current that night and Cortés was unable to row against it. He was afraid to try to land the boat onshore, fearing that it would capsize and he would drown. Instead he took off his clothes, tied them up in a bundle, which he balanced on his head, and swam to shore.

When he reached land, Cortés went directly to the home of Juan Juárez. According to his secretary, he had decided that "he wished to live in peace," and so told Juárez that he would marry Catalina. Juárez then supplied his future brother-in-law with weapons and Cortés once more hid in the church while Juárez sent word to Velázquez to intervene on Cortés's behalf.

Cortés married Catalina, but it took a bit longer to smooth over the conflict with Velázquez. In the end, they met at a farm where Velázquez was staying with some of his men. Cortés asked Velázquez to give him a full report of the accusations that had been made against him, then reassured Velázquez that he remained his supporter and friend. After a night of talking, the conflict was over and Cortés was restored to his former position of responsibility.

The experience taught Cortés that life under another man's direction was uncertain. Only in command of his own force, in areas not yet controlled by other Spaniards, would he find the power he wanted.

## Preparing for a New Adventure

Cortés was successful in his efforts to win his way back into Velázquez's good graces. This reconciliation was helped by the fact that both men were wise enough to realize the value in retaining the other as a friend rather than an enemy. Velázquez appointed Cortés as alcalde (mayor) of the town of Baracoa—a town that later became known as Santiago.

To cement his power in the region further, Velázquez was eager to oversee—and encourage—expeditions to explore and settle the surrounding lands. In 1517, one such expedition, led by Hernández de Córdoba, set sail for Yucatán, just across the sea from the western end of Cuba. Córdoba's stated goal was to explore and settle the region, although it seems clear that, like most expeditions of the time, there was also a desire to find gold and pearls. The expedition consisted of 100 men and three ships, one of which had been lent to Córdoba by Velázquez, who demanded native Indians from the lands Córdoba explored as payment for the loan.

They soon were in uncharted waters, and a storm added to the confusion. When they finally landed, they found a settlement about six miles inland that had huge, pyramid-shaped structures made of stone. They fought off an attack from the people who lived in the region and then explored these structures, discovering that they were temples to the gods of these people, which contained some gold and copper ornaments and idols. Córdoba and his men seized the objects that they thought had value, then returned to their ship and continued to sail around what they still believed to be an island, spending 15 days at sea. Each time they attempted to land, they were driven off by bands of natives. Finally, desperately in need of water, they landed, barely collecting some water before once more coming under attack by a huge force of natives. Fifty men were killed in the attack, and Córdoba himself was badly wounded. Córdoba eventually died from his injuries, but the fleet made it back to Cuba with tales of the large stone pyramids, inspiring them to refer to the place they had discovered as "Great Cairo."

Their experiences inspired wild stories and rumors in Cuba, rumors that at last a source of vast gold had been found. The accounts of fierce battles with natives were dismissed. The colonists in Cuba were accustomed to the easy victories they had experienced in their efforts to establish settlements amongst far friendlier peoples and assumed that Córdoba's men were exaggerating their experiences to make their adventures seem more heroic.

Velázquez decided that this new region, and its wealth, must be claimed as part of the territory he governed. He hired

Pyramids in Mexico were spiritual places of sacrifice to the gods. The Great Pyramid of Cholula, also known as Tlachihualtepetl (meaning "artificial mountain") is the largest monument ever constructed in the world, even larger than the Great Pyramid of Giza, in Egypt. In the second letter written to King Charles, Cortés paid tribute to the cultural and political achievements of the Aztecs, including the 400 temples he counted from the summit of the Great Pyramid.

one of his own relatives, Juan de Grijalva (his nephew), as the expedition's captain, supplied two ships of his own, and hired two of the ships that had sailed with Córdoba. The expedition set sail on May 1, 1518, and after three days discovered the island of Cozumel, on the Yucatán peninsula's eastern side. They then sailed north around Yucatán's northern tip, crossing from the Caribbean Sea into the Gulf of Mexico, and eventually landing at Champotón in the Gulf of Campeche, the very place where Córdoba's expedition had encountered its fiercest fighting and lost so many men.

Once more the Spaniards clashed with the natives. Both were prepared for the battle, the Indians with bows and arrows, lances, swords, and slingshots with stones, the Spaniards with crossbows and muskets, as well as small cannons mounted in the bows of their boats. Grijalva was injured in the battle, along with 60 of his men, but the Spaniards were able to force the Indians into retreat, occupying the region for three days before sailing on. They stayed close to the coast, trying to avoid mangrove swamps and sandbanks. Their movements were tracked by armed groups of Indians who patrolled the shores.

Grijalva and his men still believed that the Yucatán was an island. When they finally landed again, they could see Indians erecting wooden stockades and preparing for battle. Through a bit of luck, Grijalva was able to persuade them to negotiate instead, and both sides ultimately agreed to trade rather than fight. In addition to the food and water the Spaniards desperately needed, the Indians presented them with gifts of golden jewelry. According to Hammond Innes in *The Conquistadors*, the Spanish quickly asked for more gold and were told that there was none here but plenty to the west; the words *Culhúa* and *Mexico* were repeated many times.

Still seeking the end point of the "island," Grijalva and his men went back to their boats and continued sailing west. They saw settlements and towns where more warriors walked the shoreline in watchful patrol. The weather became bad, and they turned into a bay seeking shelter and saw before them the snowcapped peaks of the Sierra Madre mountains, proof at last that what they had discovered was not another island but instead the mainland of some large landmass.

They landed again near the site of the city known today as Vera Cruz, where to their surprise they were actually welcomed by the natives and were able to trade and obtain water and other supplies. At last, Grijalva formally took possession of the land they had discovered in the name of Velázquez (as the official representative of the Spanish king).

Finally, after about four months of sailing and exploring, Grijalva sent the captain of one of the ships, Pedro de Alvarado, back to Cuba with the gold they had been given in trade. He hoped that he would be able to persuade Velázquez to send reinforcements. After battling storms and mosquitoes, Grijalva and the rest of the men also decided to return to Cuba.

Grijalva had made the first efforts to explore Mexico. He returned with gold, having lost only 30 men, having successfully bartered with several of the natives he met, and having learned more about the geography of Yucatán than any explorer who had gone before him. But he would receive little recognition for his accomplishments. By the time he finally returned to Cuba, Alvarado had already preceded him with the gold and the details of what the expedition had found. Governor Velázquez was disappointed that Grijalva had not remained there to found a colony—Grijalva was falsely accused of being too cowardly to stay and fight.

In addition, political events played against Grijalva. Spain was now ruled by a young king, Charles V, who was not only ruler of Spain but also emperor of Germany. He was far more concerned with his lands in Europe than those in the distant New World. With little thought to the politics or consequences of his decisions on those governing the territories, he had decided to give the land in the Yucatán to one of his European admirals.

At the same time, Diego Columbus was claiming that he had the right to govern all lands across the ocean. When the European admiral sent five ships with settlers to begin to build a colony in Yucatán, Columbus refused to allow them to proceed. The governor in Jamaica, Francisco de Garay, was attempting to extend his governorship over additional territories in the Caribbean. Of course there was Velázquez in Cuba, who in order to strengthen his claim to the Yucatán quickly sent his personal chaplain to Spain to formally present the best of the gold Alvarado had brought back to the king.

All of these men wanted the title of governor of Yucatán, and the key seemed to lie in being the first to establish a colony there. Velázquez quickly organized an expedition with the ships and the men. Still, the expedition needed a leader, someone bold and cunning, willing to move quickly to colonize the Yucatán, even though he might not have the legal authority to do so. That man, Velázquez soon decided, was Hernán Cortés.

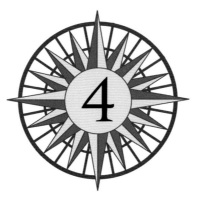

# Conquering a New Land

ON FEBRUARY 10, 1519, HERNÁN CORTÉS SET SAIL WITH MORE than 500 men and 11 ships. As discussed in the first chapter of the book, the preparations for this journey had been extensive. Cortés had left nothing to chance.

He had been specific in his instructions to the commanders of each of the 11 ships in his fleet: They were to first sail to the island of Cozumel, east of the northernmost point of the Yucatán Peninsula. Because of bad weather and the different sizes and weights of the ships in his fleet, it was inevitable that they would become separated as they sailed. So Cortés selected Cozumel as the first gathering place where the ships would come together before sailing on. According to Bernal Díaz, who sailed with Cortés and reported the details of the experience in *The Conquest of New Spain*, the ship on which he was sailing arrived two days before that of Cortés. When they explored the area while waiting for their commander, they discovered that the Indians had fled, leaving behind some turkeys and other possessions. One of the men with Díaz, Pedro de Alvarado (who had been part of Grijalva's earlier expedition), promptly seized them. They also captured three Indians who had not been able to flee to safety before the arrival of the Spanish forces.

Cortés arrived and was furious to discover that his fleet was already making enemies of the Indians. According to Díaz, he gathered the men and sternly told them that they "would never pacify the country by robbing the natives of their possessions." The captured Indians were told (by an Indian translator, Melchior, who had been taken prisoner during an earlier expedition to the region and was now accompanying Cortés) not to be afraid, but to summon the other members of their tribe. Any possessions that had been taken were returned to their owners; the turkeys that had been eaten were paid for with some beads and other trinkets. Cortés reassured the Indians that the Spaniards meant them no harm, and soon they were trading beads, bells, and other trinkets they had brought for food and some small bits of gold.

After three days on the island, Cortés decided to take stock of his supplies. The horses were brought from the ships. The islanders had never seen these animals before and stared in wonder and fear. Cortés then ordered the cannons and artillery to be tested.

The islanders approached Cortés and told him (through Melchior's translation) that two men, similar in appearance to them, had come to the island some time ago and were still alive, being held as slaves on the mainland of Yucatán. Cortés persuaded some of the islanders to go with a squadron of his men as guides and show them the place where the Spaniards were being held prisoner. He sent two armed ships—the smallest of his fleet—to the place the islanders had indicated: Cape Catoche, some 12 miles from Cozumel.

While the rescue mission was dispatched, Cortés began exploring Cozumel further. He discovered that the homes were

well built, and that the natives had a complex system of record-
ing events using drawings on stretched bark. He was especially
interested in the temple, a large, pyramid-shaped structure built
of limestone with an open space at the top that overlooked the
sea. This open space was covered with bones and bloodstains,
and Cortés learned that the islanders gathered here to pray for
rain and to sacrifice animals and people to the gods.

Cortés gathered the leaders of the tribe and told them
they must dispose of the evil idols, urging them instead to embrace the one God of the Christian faith. According to Díaz,
the islanders refused, explaining that even their ancestors had
worshipped these gods, they were good, and if the Spaniards
insulted them they would die. Cortés dramatically ordered his
men to destroy the idols and roll them down the steps of the
pyramid, scrub away the bloodstains from the sacrifices, and
set up an altar with a wooden cross and a small statue of the
Virgin Mary. He then told the islanders that they must worship
here instead.

The expedition to find the rumored Spaniard prisoners
returned without having recovered the men. Cortés finally ordered his fleet to set sail for Isla Mujeres, an island discovered
by Francisco de Córdoba two years earlier. One of the ships
quickly began to leak; Cortés ordered the fleet to return to
Cozumel where they worked to caulk the leaks, helped by the
islanders. While the ship was being repaired, Cortés once more
ordered that the ammunition be unloaded and tested.

As they prepared to set sail again, a canoe appeared off the
coast, paddling toward them from the mainland. There were
six men, armed with bows and arrows, in the canoe. One of
them stood as the Spaniards approached and spoke to them
in clumsy Spanish. It was a Spanish priest named Jerónimo de
Aguilar, who had been shipwrecked off the coast of Jamaica in
1511. He and about 20 others gradually washed ashore on the
Yucatán peninsula. Only a handful had survived the trip; they

The worship of idols was central to the Aztec religious, social, and political practices. Statues in the shapes of animals, people, or things in nature were the physical representations of gods. The gods were in control of the forces of nature. Believing that he was presenting them with "the true faith," Cortés destroyed the Aztec idols and told them to end their practice of human sacrifice and cannibalism.

were quickly taken prisoner by the Mayan tribesman who found them. Aguilar and a few of the others were crammed into a wooden cage and forced to watch as five of their comrades were sacrificed and eaten. They were able to break out of their cage and quickly slipped away in the night, ending up in a village where they were made slaves. Aguilar became known as "the white slave," who through luck and hard work survived eight years in service, finally winning his freedom. He had learned of the arrival of the Spanish rescue mission, and had come across the water to join them.

His arrival was a real stroke of luck for Cortés. During his eight years as a slave, Aguilar had become fluent in the Chontal Mayan spoken in the Yucatán. He also had lived among the people and understood their customs and habits. His Spanish had become a bit rusty from disuse, but it was still far better than the fragments spoken by Melchior. Aguilar was appointed Cortés's official translator, and the expedition set out again for the Yucatán mainland.

## Exploring the Coastline

The fleet set out on March 4, 1519. Much of this area had previously been explored by Grijalva and Córdoba. When they reached a point near Champotón, where both Córdoba and Grijalva had encountered fierce fighting and lost many men, Cortés debated landing. According to Díaz, "Cortés was anxious to pay the Indians out for the defeats they had inflicted . . . and many of us soldiers who had taken part in those battles begged him to go in and give them a good punishment." But the fleet had already encountered rough weather—making it difficult to keep the ships together or relatively close to each other—and some of the pilots urged Cortés to sail on while the weather was good.

On March 12, 1519, they reached their next landing point, the mouth of a river Grijalva had named after himself and which the Indians called the Tabasco River. They transferred to smaller boats and rowed up the river, heading for the town of Tabasco. When Grijalva had landed there, the natives had been friendly and given him gold, but Cortés discovered that the mood had definitely changed. The bank of the river was crowded with armed warriors, and according to Díaz more than 12,000 had gathered in the town in preparation for an attack on the Spaniards.

Cortés sent in Aguilar to try to negotiate so that they could trade for food and water, but the people refused. Apparently they had been taunted by their neighbors—the people of Champotón—for failing to fight with Grijalva's men and had been sufficiently humiliated. They resolved never again to deal with the Spaniards. Instead, they wanted to fight.

Battle soon followed. According to Díaz, "the whole bank was thick with Indian warriors, carrying their native arms, blowing trumpets and conches, and beating drums." Cortés made one more appeal, through Aguilar, for peaceful negotiation. The response was a volley of arrows and fierce drumbeats. Many got into canoes and rowed toward the Spaniards, shooting more arrows. The Spaniards, attempting to land, were caught in mud and water, in some places up to their waists. Cortés lost a shoe in the mud, finally fighting his way to shore with one bare foot.

The artillery of the Spaniards ultimately proved too much for the Indians. Cortés and his men fought their way into the town of Tabasco, taking possession of the land for the king of Spain. Once more Cortés sealed his efforts with a dramatic gesture: He drew his sword and, walking over to a large tree that stood in the center of the town's main courtyard, he marked the tree with three sweeping slashes of his sword. He then called out that any who objected to the claim of the king would have to face him—and his sword.

Fourteen of Cortés's men had been injured in the fight; Díaz himself was shot in the thigh by an arrow. Eighteen Indians died in the battle.

Shortly after the battle, Melchior (the original interpreter) deserted. The Indians then massed again for another attack. Cortés had been able to bring his horses ashore, and although they were stiff from their long confinement onboard the ship they were outfitted with steel breastplates and bells were attached to them.

A far larger group of Indians faced the Spaniard this time—they were outnumbered roughly 300 to one. "All the men wore great feather crests," Díaz later reported, "they carried drums and trumpets, their faces were painted black and white, they were armed with large bows and arrows, spears and shields, swords like our two-handed swords, and slings and stones and fire-toughened darts, and all wore quilted cotton armour. Their squadrons, as they approached us, were so numerous that they covered the whole savannah." When the Spaniards fired upon them, the Indians would throw dirt up into the air so the Spaniards could not see whether or not they had hit their targets.

It was the cavalry that proved critical in this battle. The Indians had never seen trained horses before, and some, according to Díaz, feared that the horse and rider were one creature. They fled before the cavalry, and the battle ended.

In addition to the many killed, five Indians had been captured, including two chiefs. Cortés decided to use diplomacy, inspired in part by the fact that the Indians had a clear advantage in numbers. There was no way that the Spaniards could hope to establish settlements in Yucatán by force. They would need to negotiate.

Cortés released the captives and sent them back with some small gifts, telling them that he came in peace and asking them to carry this message to the tribal leaders. Soon, a group of slaves in ragged clothes and blackened faces came back to Cortés with a gift of food, but Aguilar told the slaves that Cortés would only deal with their leaders.

Thirty of the leaders returned the next day. These leaders were dressed in fine cloaks and carried fowls, fish, fruit, and cakes made of maize. They asked Cortés for his permission to burn and bury their dead—they had lost some 800 men—to prevent them from being eaten by lions or tigers. Cortés agreed.

Sensing that the horses had proved his most critical weapon, he then decided to demonstrate his power to these tribal leaders. A mare was hidden in the spot behind where the tribal leaders were taken. Cortés then stood before them and sternly explained that they and their land now belonged to the Spanish king. At his signal, a cannon was fired and a large stallion was brought before the leaders. The stallion could sense that the mare was somewhere behind the leaders, and so it stood staring in their direction, pawing the ground and neighing.

Hammond Innes in *The Conquistadors* describes this scene as "very childish, very theatrical; but it was nevertheless a most effective demonstration of power, with his men all about him, rank on rank and armed, and the ships riding off the land. . . . The result was peace and a plentiful supply of food."

Cortés knew that the scene would carry a message far beyond those who witnessed it. He suspected that the tribes along the Yucatán communicated, both through picture writing and messengers, and that word of the mighty army would spread to other tribes in the region.

Next, Cortés told the leaders to gather their people in the center of town. He assured them of his peaceful intentions and, as he had done before, he ordered them to abandon their idols. Cortés was interested not only in converting them to Christianity, but he understood that by eliminating the symbols that connected them to their past and their ancestors, replacing them with an altar and a cross, he would create an environment of uncertainty and fear.

Once again Cortés brought up the question of gold. Again he heard the replies, "Culhúa" and "Mexico." The people

Doña Marina, also known as La Malinche, was a young noble-woman from the Nahua tribe in central Mexico. She helped Cortés in his conquest of the Aztecs by serving as his interpreter, adviser, and intermediary. Later she bore him a son. Today, some people see her as a traitor to her people, while others regard her as a hero. Here, Doña Marina introduces the blind king of Tlaxcala to Cortés.

presented Cortés with 20 women. Among them was a woman who would play a critical role in the expedition. This one woman was given the name Doña Marina. (Her real name was Malinche.) She would ultimately become the wife of one of Cortés's men and quickly learned Spanish. Doña Marina spoke Náhuatl, the language of the Aztecs of Culhúa and Mexico, as well as Tabascan. Aguilar, the official translator, spoke only Tabascan. As Cortés and his crew moved deeper inland, Doña

## DOÑA MARINA

The story of Cortés' translator Doña Marina is an amazing tale of a young Indian princess who was presented to Cortés as a servant and instead became critical to his success.

The young woman who would later be given the Spanish name Marina was the daughter of two Indian rulers in the town of Paynala. Her given name was Malinche. Her father died when she was young; her mother remarried and had a son with her new husband. Her mother and stepfather then decided that their son would be their official heir and rule after their death. To ensure that this happened, they sold the young girl to some Indians from a distant town, who smuggled her from her home one night. The royal couple then claimed that the girl had died.

She was taken to Tabasco, where she lived as a slave until Cortés's arrival. The Tabascans then gave her to Cortés. She eventually married one of his men.

Her royal upbringing stayed with her. Bernal Díaz, in his memoir *The Conquest of New Spain*, writes that she "was a person of great importance, and was obeyed without question by all the Indians of New Spain." She quickly learned Spanish and her fluency in the language spoken by the Aztecs made

*(Continues)*

*(Continued)*

her a critical part of Cortés's expedition. She was given the title "Doña," or "Lady," in recognition of her royal background and as a sign of respect for her importance to Cortés.

Cortés eventually reached the town where Doña Marina had lived as a little girl. When Cortés summoned the rulers and leaders of the community, Doña Marina's mother and half brother were in the group. They were terrified when they saw her with Cortés, fearing that they would be executed.

Doña Marina saw their fear—and their tears—and told them not to be afraid. She told her mother that she forgave her and presented her with clothes and jewels. She then sent the two back to their town.

Throughout Cortés's journey of conquest, he frequently relied on Doña Marina to communicate with the people he encountered. As Bernal Díaz noted, the arrival of Doña Marina was "the great beginning of our conquests . . . without Doña Marina we could not have understood the language of New Spain and Mexico."

Marina would play an increasingly important role in translating. At first, she translated the Náhuatl of the people they encountered in Tabascan and Aguilar would translate it into Spanish. Eventually, as Doña Marina's Spanish grew more fluent, she replaced Aguilar as the translator for Cortés.

## The First Mention of Montezuma

After their victory at Tabasco, Cortés and his crew set sail, landing after four days at San Juan de Ulúa, where a group of Indians paddled out in two canoes to greet them. They announced that they had been sent by their ruler, who wanted to find out who the strangers were and what they wanted. Their leader—a man named Tendile—served the great Montezuma.

It was the first time Cortés heard the name of the Aztec leader with whom his destiny would become linked. He

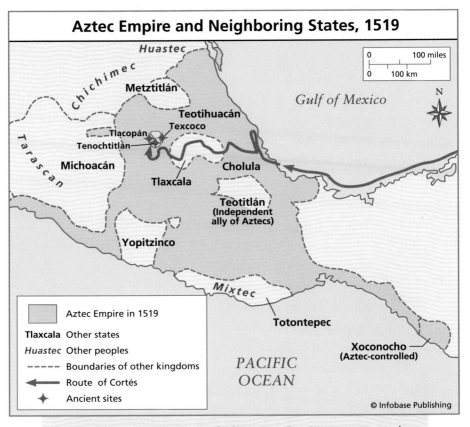

## Aztec Empire and Neighboring States, 1519

Huastec

Chichimec

Metztitlán

Teotihuacán

Texcoco

Tlacopán

Tenochtitlán

Tarascan

Michoacán

Tlaxcala

Cholula

Teotitlán
(Independent
ally of Aztecs)

Yopitzinco

Mixtec

Totontepec

Xoconocho
(Aztec-controlled)

Gulf of Mexico

N

PACIFIC
OCEAN

0        100 miles
0      100 km

Aztec Empire in 1519
**Tlaxcala** Other states
*Huastec* Other peoples
- - - - - Boundaries of other kingdoms
← Route of Cortés
✦ Ancient sites

© Infobase Publishing

At the time of Cortés's arrival, the Aztec Empire encompassed a region stretching from central Mexico to the Gulf of Mexico to the east and the border of Guatemala to the south. By 1519, Tenochtitlán was the largest city in the world. The Mexican people of Tenochtitlán formed a triple alliance with the city-states of Texcoco and Tlacopan. The other city-states, which were made up of different ethnic groups, were forced to pay tribute to the alliance.

understood that his arrival would be reported, in detail, and decided to make sure that the details were suitably impressive.

Cortés explained that he had come to trade, and that his intentions were peaceful. When the Indians offered gifts of crafts made with feathers, some cotton garments, and small gold trinkets, Cortés gave them food, wine, metal tools, and some blue glass beads. Cortés asked the men to take the wine to their leader, Tendile, explaining that he would like to meet him.

Cortés then had half of his force—about 200 soldiers—land onshore, along with the horses and artillery. The men set up camp on a sand dune and stationed their cannons and artillery on the dunes.

By the next day, more Indians arrived, explaining that they, too, were ruled over by the great Montezuma whose kingdom, they explained, was "Mexico," a territory connecting the city-states of Tenochtitlán, Texcoco, and Tacuba. (While they described the kingdom as Mexico, we know it today as the Aztec kingdom.) They presented Cortés with more gifts of feather and gold crafts, as well as food.

Within a few days, the governor Tendile himself arrived, accompanied by several thousand men. He bowed humbly to Cortés, and presented him with a fine chest containing golden objects, jewelry, and 10 bales of white cloth made of cotton and feathers. There was also food—fruit, fish, and fowls. He had brought painters with him. They were instructed to make portraits of Cortés, his captains and soldiers, the ships, the cannons, and the horses. They quickly began drawing on a large canvas made from dried plant. These portraits were ultimately carried to Montezuma.

Cortés then presented Tendile with a red Spanish cap, embroidered in gold, showing a mounted soldier killing a dragon. He also gave Tendile a gift that he said was for Montezuma—a carved Spanish armchair upon which, Cortés said, Montezuma might sit when they met. Cortés told Tendile that he, too, served a distant king, one who lived far across the waters to the east and one who (Cortés lied) had sent him specifically to meet personally with Montezuma. He then decided to put on a display for the sketch artists.

Cortés ordered the cannons to be loaded and his cavalry to mount their horses. Cortés himself mounted his horse, and led his men away from the dunes and down to the shoreline. The tide was low and the horses could gallop on firmer ground through the water. The cannons were fired, and Cortés and his men put on a military display complete with charging horses churning up the water, bells ringing, and swords flashing.

Tendile and his men had never seen such a display. Tendile was particularly interested in the helmet worn by one of the Spanish soldiers. It was made of metal, with a peak that sloped from front to back. Tendile said that the helmet resembled that worn by their war gods, specifically the gods Huitzilopochtli and Quetzalcoatl. Tendile asked Cortés if he might have this helmet to show to Montezuma. Cortés replied that he could take the helmet, if it was returned filled with Aztec gold that he could then give to his own king.

Cortés's secretary, Francisco López de Gómara, reported that Cortés told Tendile, "I and my companions suffer from a disease of the heart which can be cured only with gold." In *Cortés: The Life of the Conqueror by His Secretary*, Gómara wrote that the message and paintings were swiftly conveyed to Montezuma through a kind of relay system. Indian guards were stationed at regular intervals from the coast all the way to Montezuma's palace, and the news of Cortés's arrival, the gifts, and the paintings were passed hand to hand.

Cortés and his men settled into their camp on the beach to await Montezuma's reply. Some six or seven days passed. The men were well fed and more Indians arrived with goods to trade.

Finally, Tendile returned with some 100 Indians, as well as a Mexican chief who bore a startling resemblance to Cortés, named Qunitalbor. Montezuma had apparently chosen him because of this resemblance, which had been clear to him as soon as he had seen the sketches the artists had prepared.

The men with Tendile immediately began perfuming the air with incense carried in earthen pots. Quintalbor then presented Cortés with an impressive collection of gifts from Montezuma. There was an engraved disk in the shape of the sun, as big as a cartwheel and made from gold. There was a larger engraved disk in the shape of the moon, made from fine silver. There were 20 ducks carved from gold, as well as ornaments in the shapes of dogs, tigers, lions, deer, and monkeys. There were necklaces, bow and arrows, and crests all made of fine gold. There were 30 bales of cotton cloth, decorated with multicolored feathers. And there was the Spanish helmet, filled with small grains of gold.

It was a display as impressive as Cortés's military exercises, intended to demonstrate the wealth and power of Montezuma. Montezuma had also sent a message: He welcomed Cortés and his men to his country, praising them for their victory at Tabasco. He would be happy to serve them in any way he could while they were in his country. But he had no wish to meet with them personally, and they were not to travel inland to visit him. Instead, they should take the wonderful gifts they had been given and leave.

Montezuma's gifts were intended to show the vast wealth of his kingdom, and in this they were successful. The Spaniards had never seen such fine gold, much of the craftsmanship far superior to anything that existed in Europe. It was greed, not fear, which was triggered by Montezuma's display.

Cortés thanked Tendile for the gifts and repeated his request to meet with Montezuma personally. He scraped together whatever suitable gifts he could find to offer Montezuma—some shirts made of fine linen, a glass goblet engraved with hunting scenes, and some glass beads. Then he waited for Montezuma's reply.

# In the Land of Montezuma

CORTÉS AND HIS MEN SETTLED INTO THEIR CAMP TO WAIT FOR Montezuma's reply. It was an unpleasant setting—the sandy beach was hot and humid and mosquitoes buzzed around the men. The Indians, who had initially been welcoming, came less often and food supplies ran low. The Indians were alarmed by the religious practices of the Spaniards and by Cortés's suggestion that he had been sent by his king to destroy the Indians' idols. They were puzzled by the Spaniards' constant requests for gold and finally they stopped coming to the camp altogether.

Cortés sent a crew of his men in two ships to scout the coast to the north. They traveled up to the Pánuco River, some 50 miles further north than Grijalva had explored, reaching the place where the port city of Tampico is now located. They returned to Cortés with reports of a town some 36 miles away called Quiahuitztlan.

Finally, Tendile returned with more gifts of gold and with Montezuma's reply. He would not meet Cortés.

During Montezuma's reign, the ninth Aztec emperor and high priest expanded the empire to its maximum size before it was defeated. In fact, the empire had gotten too big so Montezuma strengthened his authority over the independent city-states and enforced a more centralized government. This included the powerful Tlaxcalans, a group Montezuma had never been able to conquer.

As Cortés decided what to do next, he became aware of a growing dissatisfaction among his men. Those with homes and families in Cuba were anxious to return. They now had a fortune in gold, far more than any other expedition had obtained, and they had explored further along the north coast.

Montezuma had given instructions that his people should have no further dealings with Cortés and his men. The atmosphere in the camp began to change. Cortés sensed a new hostility from the Indians. He instructed his men to prepare for an attack.

Into this tense atmosphere, a group of five Indians from the Totonac tribe appeared and approached Cortés. They explained that they were from the town of Zempoala. Their physical appearance was different from the people of Culhúa. They had holes in their lower lips in which had been placed disks of stone or gold, as did the holes in their ears. They bowed to Cortés and murmured the words "Lope luzio, lope luzio." With the aid of Doña Marina, Cortés learned that the greeting was "Prince and great lord." They explained that they had waited until the people of Culhúa were gone before they had ventured into the camp. They praised Cortés for his victories in Tabasco and Champotón.

It became clear to Cortés that the men were not friendly with the Culhúans. Cortés sensed an opportunity. These people might be interested in an alliance—an alliance that could ultimately be used against Montezuma—by picking off bits of his kingdom a little at a time. Cortés knew that the Spaniards, in their current state, could not successfully conquer Montezuma's kingdom by force. If he could increase the size of his army by adding Indians dissatisfied with Montezuma's rule, he might indeed be able to build a more suitable army.

Cortés presented the men with gifts and asked them to tell their leader he would soon visit. He then set out with most of his men, leaving only a small number behind to guard the camp. They marched for several miles away from the coast and into the country, finally coming upon several small settlements with homes made of adobe and thatch, all recently abandoned. Cortés announced to the men that anyone who looted the homes would be executed. He needed the goodwill of these people in order for his plan to succeed.

## MONTEZUMA

The ruler of Mexico, Montezuma (also known as Moctezuma), was actually Montezuma II (the first Montezuma had been his great-grandfather, who had ruled in the mid-fifteenth century). *Montezuma* means "he who angers himself." He had become emperor following the reign of his uncle, who had died in 1502. He was about 22 years old when he became the leader of the Aztecs. Montezuma had served as an Aztec priest before becoming ruler, and his religious beliefs would remain central for the rest of his life.

In Aztec custom emperors did not pass the throne from father to son. Instead a select group of 12 advisers met after the death of a ruler to determine which family member was most qualified to rule—a kind of electoral college who picked the new emperor and then would become his chief council. All members of the family were prepared to rule. They were expected to perform heroically in battle and serve in the Aztec temple in some capacity. Montezuma II, the eighth son of the brother of the king, was found to be the most qualified family member when the king died in 1502.

Montezuma is believed to have been born in 1480, five years before Cortés. He was of average height, with dark hair that came about to his shoulders and a short black beard. He was described by Bernal Díaz and others who met him as clever and wise. His voice was firm but low and his speeches were considered to be very eloquent. He was polite and diplomatic; prior to the arrival of the Spaniards, much of Montezuma's governing had focused on lengthy meetings with the

In the village they found a small temple, accessed by 20 steps. According to Cortés's secretary, Gómara, "a great many bits of paper . . . soaked in blood, were strewn about, and there was much blood from sacrificed men . . . and a block on which the victims were stretched for sacrifice, and flint knives with which they were cut open, while their hearts were torn out."

leaders who sought his advice or decisions of disputes and matters of state. Those who were granted a meeting were expected to avoid eye contact with him and to speak very quietly.

Montezuma had a large family with several wives. It is estimated that he had anywhere from 19 to 150 children. As a way to demonstrate his wealth and the splendor of his kingdom, he would change his clothing four times a day, never wearing the same tunic more than once.

Under Montezuma the Aztec kingdom expanded as new territory was conquered. These conquered territories were not consolidated into a whole in the same way that a country or empire is recognized in modern times. Instead, these new territories remained somewhat independent. They were expected to pay regular taxes or tributes to Montezuma, but for the most part their local leaders were allowed to continue to govern. This situation enabled Cortés to quickly form alliances with some of the more discontented parts of Montezuma's empire and to persuade them to pay tribute to the Spanish king instead.

Montezuma also oversaw an expansion of the creation of works of art, especially stone carving. Design work done with feathers also flourished during his rule.

The Aztec kingdom stretched through most of Mexico and Central America. The capital was Tenochtitlán, near the site of present-day Mexico City. At the height of his power, Montezuma ruled over some 5 million people.

Almost from the time he had ascended to the throne, word had come to Montezuma of strange men—men whose skin was white and whose ships were as large as palaces. There were rumors of gods coming back to reclaim their lands, and of evil omens of the world coming to an end.

Cortés returned to his camp to discover his men openly divided. Many of those who had remained at the beach were arguing to return to Cuba. He then called a meeting, inviting selected members of his crew to voice their opinions. Cortés had cleverly chosen so that most of the invited men at the meeting supported the idea of continuing the expedition. He invited those there to speak, and most argued forcefully that there must be even more wealth to be found in this land. By appearing to listen to his men, and then inviting them to vote, he made it seem that he was following their wishes when those in attendance loudly voted for continuing.

Cortés then announced that he would resign the commission he had been given by Velázquez—the commission that had been the reason for the expedition. Instead, he and his men would found a legal settlement where they were camped. This humble beach camp would become the site of the colony Villa Rica de la Vera Cruz (the Rich Town of the True Cross). Cortés had legal documents drawn up that created a government—a government whose officers (including a notary, judge, councilors, and a constable) were his most loyal men. Then, calling upon his men to elect a chief justice and captain-general of this new settlement, Cortés dramatically walked out of the meeting. Within moments, his men had elected Cortés to both positions.

According to Buddy Levy in *Conquistador*, Cortés's actions in this encounter demonstrated his skill for diplomacy and his awareness of the importance of legal status. By resigning his commission and founding a town, Cortés was publicly declaring that he was no longer under the authority of Velázquez. As the leader of a new Spanish colony, Cortés now answered only to the authority of the Spanish king, Charles V. Within a few days, Cortés began to send a series of letters to his new boss explaining his actions and promising to his king a vast new territory.

# Relocating the Camp

When the men who had argued for returning to Cuba discovered what had happened, they protested. The loudest were arrested. Others that Cortés suspected of plotting against him were sent on scouting missions inland, to keep them from persuading the others to join them. Cortés next decided to move his base camp further inland to the town of Quiahuitztlan, which had been discovered by one of the scouting teams. The men began marching up the coast, finally arriving at the Totonac town of Cempoala.

Cempoala was a welcome change from the heat and mosquitoes of their beach camp. Bernal Díaz described it as "so green with vegetation that it looked like a garden." It was the largest town Cortés and his men had found on their voyage, and the streets were crowded with Indians who had come to see them. The plaster of the buildings was cleaned and scrubbed to a shining silver. The leader of the town welcomed Cortés, bowing to him and bringing him and his men baskets of plums and cakes made of maize. The hungry men quickly dubbed the town Villa Viciosa, meaning "city of abundance," while others named it for the Spanish city of Seville.

The town leader, or *cacique*, greeted Cortés with "Lope luzio" and presented him with gifts of gold and cloth. He quickly began criticizing Montezuma, explaining that Montezuma had recently enslaved the people of Cempoala, had robbed them of their jewelry, had taken their sons away to be sacrificed and helped himself to their wives and daughters.

Cortés was quite happy to hear this, sensing again a weakness in Montezuma's empire and an opportunity for a useful alliance. He told the cacique that he was planning to settle in the town of Quiahuitztlan, and once there he would carefully consider what the cacique had told him. For good measure, he added a few remarks about the great king across the sea whom he served, and how he (Cortés) had been sent to bring an end to the sacrifice of the cacique's people.

The following day, Cortés and his men continued their journey to the Indian town of Quiahuitztlan. When they arrived there, they found it nearly deserted. In the center of the town, where the temples were located, they found 15 priests who welcomed them and told them that the people had fled in fear because of the Spaniards, particularly their horses. Cortés had barely begun his standard speech—asking them to call back their people, explaining that he came in peace and that he served a great emperor across the sea who had sent him to bring an end to the practice of human sacrifice and robbery—when he was interrupted by the cacique of Cempoala. He had apparently followed Cortés and his men. The cacique was carried into the center of town on a litter (a kind of elaborate couch) placed on the shoulders of several strong men.

The cacique of Cempoala then joined the cacique of Quiahuitztlan and the men began to jointly complain about the unjust actions of Montezuma. While they were describing in detail the horrors of Montezuma's oversight—their goods being robbed from them, their children taken away as human sacrifices—messengers rushed in with news. Five of Montezuma's tax collectors were on their way to the town. The caciques, who only moments before had been complaining of Montezuma's actions, were terrified. They quickly ordered that a room be prepared for the tax collectors, with flowers, food, and their finest drink: cocoa.

Bernal Díaz describes the dramatic arrival of Montezuma's tax collectors. They moved arrogantly into the center of town, walking past Cortés and his men without even acknowledging their presence. They wore richly embroidered cloaks and carried roses, which they periodically sniffed. They were accompanied by servants whose job was to whisk away any flies that might dare to swoop too near.

They were led to their room. After they had eaten, they ordered the caciques to come before them and began to scold them for allowing the Spaniards to enter their town. The tax collectors then demanded 20 men and women from their villages to serve as sacrifices to the gods for the mistake the caciques had made.

Doña Marina was nearby, translating all of this for Cortés. As soon as he heard what was happening, he quickly called the caciques to his room. He reminded them that the Spanish king had sent Cortés to bring an end to these kinds of sacrifices and robbery. Cortés told the caciques to arrest the tax collectors and send out messengers to all of the nearby villages. They were to tell what they had done so that those people, too, would stop paying tribute to Montezuma.

Emboldened by the presence of the armed Spaniards, the caciques eventually ordered the messengers to go out and the people of Quiahuitztlan seized the tax collectors and tied them to long poles. The caciques then suggested that the tax collectors be sacrificed, but Cortés had a far more intricate plan. He wanted not only to form an alliance with these people, but he wanted to sharpen the divide between them and Montezuma so that they would be forced to side with the Spanish.

Cortés instructed the Totonacs to place the Aztec tax collectors in a room. He then told them that he would assign his best men as guards. Late in the night, when the Totonacs were gone, Cortés ordered the guards to release two of the tax collectors and bring them to him. Cortés questioned them with Doña Marina's help, pretending shock at what had occurred and explaining that the Totonacs had acted independently. He told the men that he had already exchanged gifts with their leader, Montezuma, and was horrified to find his men being treated so roughly.

Cortés gave the men something to eat and drink and offered to help them escape, provided that they would tell

Montezuma that Cortés had done this as a gesture of goodwill and in a desire for peace. He then ordered several guards to smuggle the men out of the town.

The next day, the Totonacs were furious when they learned that two of their prisoners had escaped. Cortés pretended to share their anger. He promised to increase the security around the remaining three tax collectors. He had them put in chains and marched to the river, where they were placed on small boats and rowed out to sea.

Meanwhile, back in Quiahuitztlan, the Totonacs were in a bind. They had already informed all of the neighboring villages of their actions. The tax collectors were certain to go back to Montezuma and report their treachery. There was little doubt that Montezuma would retaliate. Facing certain annihilation, they had little choice but to sign a treaty committing themselves to join with Cortés, obey his instructions, and cooperate in his fight against Montezuma. With his act of trickery, Cortés gained the district—some 20 towns—for the Spanish crown.

He also planned the site of what would become the first Spanish settlement. He began building the fortress near the river, about a mile and a half from Quiahuitztlan. Cortés helped with the actual construction of the foundation, inspiring all of his men to join in the work. Plans were begun for a church, a plaza, weapons arsenals, and watchtowers. The Totonacs helped with the construction, and by June 28, 1519, Vera Cruz had been founded.

During the construction, emissaries from Montezuma arrived, bringing more gifts. When they asked Cortés to explain the ill treatment of the tax collectors, Cortés replied that the Totonacs now served the Spanish king and so could not be expected to also pay taxes to Montezuma. Then he produced the remaining three tax collectors, who had been well fed during their captivity, and promised to visit Montezuma in the future.

Shortly after this contingent left, the cacique from Cempoala arrived, once more carried on the shoulders of his men. He told Cortés that Aztecs were attacking Totonac villages in retaliation for what had happened in Quiahuitztlan. Cortés needed to honor the treaty that had been signed and come to their aid.

Cortés quickly assembled a squadron of his best men and rode to the place where the cacique had told him the attacks were happening. When he arrived, he quickly found that it was actually Totonacs attacking other Totonacs, looting their supplies, and kidnapping their women and children. All of this was part of an ongoing and long-lasting dispute over boundaries. There were no Aztecs involved.

Cortés rode back to his camp and the next day called a meeting of all the chiefs of the neighboring towns. He then laid out the conditions that must prevail in order for him to help them and keep the peace: They must stop fighting with each other, and they must give up the practice of human sacrifice and stop worshipping idols.

The people protested; their idols, they believed, had protected them and provided them with good weather, good harvests, and long life. Still Cortés was firm. To emphasize his determination, he had an armed guard of 50 soldiers march forward to the bottom steps of the temple with their swords drawn. Cortés then seized the cacique of Cempoala and put a sword to his throat. He explained that, unless his soldiers were allowed to proceed with the destruction of the idols, the cacique and all of their priests would be killed.

The cacique quickly ordered his men to put down their bows and spears, and the 50 soldiers marched up the temple steps. The great stone idols that stood at the top were thrown down the steps, where they broke into pieces. The Totonacs immediately began to call out in fear, begging the gods to forgive them. The priests were ordered to take away the scraps and burn them.

Cortés then ordered the temple to be scrubbed in order to remove the bloodstains and evidence of sacrifice. Incense was burned to remove the smell of blood and an altar was built, covered with fine linen. A vase of roses was placed on top. The priests who had cared for the temple were now instructed to care for these symbols of the new faith. Their hair (which had been so long it nearly touched the ground) was cut, and they were given new white robes to wear. A mass was said, and the people looked on in wonder, amazed that the destruction of the idols had not led to some clear sign of anger from their gods.

## Letters from Mexico

Back in Vera Cruz, Cortés decided that he needed to cement his position in what he called "New Spain." He had spent about three months exploring the coast. He wanted to move inland. Critical to his success was the support of the Spanish king. He needed to make it clear to King Charles that any territories discovered would be governed by him, not by Velázquez or any of the other men aspiring to be governor of any newly discovered lands.

Cortés explained to his men the urgency of this effort. Then, he told them that all of the treasure they had obtained— the gold, the jewelry, the elaborate cloth and featherwork— must be loaded onto a ship and sent to King Charles. Many of the men were furious. The king was only entitled to one-fifth of what they had found. Instead they were being asked to give all of it up.

Cortés reminded them that they had consistently been told that the greatest supply of gold lay in Mexico. Certainly, he argued, Montezuma would keep the greatest treasure where he lived. More, and far better, things lay ahead, but first they must win the support of the king to proceed with the expedition. And to win his support, they had to impress him with treasure far greater than any other expedition had obtained.

Cortés wrote a detailed letter, outlining in detail all of their experiences so far. There would eventually be five of these letters, sent over a seven-year period to King Charles. Known as the *Letters from Mexico*, they provide an in-depth account from Cortés's perspective of what he saw and did, with a heavy emphasis on his loyalty to the king. In the first letter, Cortés also made it clear why he, and not Velázquez, should be the governor of these newly discovered lands.

Cortés then ordered the gold and treasure to be placed on his best ship. He selected two of his most experienced captains and ordered them to guard with their lives the treasure and the letter to the king. He also gave them copies of the legal documents that founded Vera Cruz and ended the trading agreement with Velázquez. On July 26, the ship set sail under orders to travel to Spain as fast as possible.

## Burning the Ships

Many of the men were furious at their treasure being sent off, and their discontent grew as they realized that Cortés planned not to return to Cuba but to march inland. Plans for a mutiny spread, and a group of men began to stockpile supplies of salt pork, bread, water, oil, and fish. They intended to take one of the smaller boats and slip away silently at midnight, sail after the treasure ship, capture it, and return it to Velázquez in Cuba.

Cortés learned of the plot and recognized that, as long as there were ships to be seized and dissatisfied men, there was a danger of his expedition collapsing. The plotters were arrested, and the man identified as the leader of the mutiny was hanged.

Cortés ordered several of his most trusted men to drill holes in the bottom of all of the boats in his fleet. Then he announced to the men that the boat hulls had been eaten by worms and were no longer seaworthy. He ordered the men to strip the boats of sails and ropes, oars, all navigational

The men still loyal to Velázquez conspired to seize a ship and sail back to Cuba. To prevent desertion by his men, Cortés sank 10 of his own ships, under the pretext that they were not seaworthy. The men had no choice but to follow Cortés on his quest to conquer the Aztecs.

equipment, and any necessary supplies. This was stored in the fort at Vera Cruz.

Cortés then ordered all of the ships to be sunk. As the horrified men watched, the fleet that represented their only way to return home slowly slipped below the water.

Now there was no way out. The men had one choice: conquer or be conquered.

# Into the Heart of the Aztec Kingdom

On August 16, 1519, CORTÉS SET OUT INTO THE HEART OF THE Aztec kingdom. Some 150 men were left behind (including those who were sick and wounded) to guard Vera Cruz and continue the construction on the settlement. This left some 400 Spaniards who would accompany Cortés on the journey. The Indians had also agreed to supply Cortés with several of their best warriors and some porters to help transport equipment.

There were mountains visible in the distance, so Cortés's preparations needed to take into account a journey that might be difficult and uphill. This meant abandoning the heavier cannons. Wheeled wooden carts were constructed to help transport some of the heavy artillery and equipment.

Cortés wanted his men to be prepared for battle at all times. The soldiers were instructed to constantly wear their best armor—even to sleep in it—and to carry their weapons. Cortés rode on horseback at the head of the cavalry.

Cortés and his men were facing a journey of about 250 miles to the Aztec capital. No Spaniard had traveled there before, so the territory was completely unknown. They would need to cross three large mountain ranges, and the full extent of Montezuma's army was still a mystery.

They headed first for Jalapa, a fairly large town that lay at the base of the first great mountain range. It was at the limit of Totonac territory, so for the first few days Cortés and his

At the bottom of the Orizaba Mountains was an important town at the time of the conquest. An estimated 1.5 million people that live in the nearby towns still speak a variant of Náhuatl, the language of the Aztecs.

men moved through friendly people and had plenty to eat. In *Conquistador*, Buddy Levy notes that the forests through which they marched contained jaguars and ocelots. Parrots and macaws called out around them. There were fragrant clusters of cacao and vanilla plants. To the southwest they could see the snowcapped dome of Orizaba Mountain, which at nearly 19,000 feet above sea level, was twice as high as any mountain in Spain.

The weather grew cooler as they climbed the mountain, even though it was still summer. There were two paths cut into the mountain, leading up the rocks. They came upon a few simple dwellings, made from gray adobe, before descending into what Cortés's secretary, Gómara, described as a "desert country, uninhabited and saline," where the water was salty. They also encountered cold weather and a sandstorm. Some of the Cubans who had accompanied them died at this stage, unaccustomed to the sudden cold and lacking proper clothing and blankets.

Finally, after several more days of marching, they reached a large town where the homes made of stone gleamed white in the sunlight. They named it "Castilblanco"—its Indian name was Xocotlán. There they were welcomed by the chief cacique, who told them Montezuma had given his people instructions not to harm them as they journeyed through his lands. The cacique also described the Aztec capital, known both as "Mexico" and "Tenochtitlán." He told them that the houses there were built on water, all paths into the city were guarded by drawbridges, and there were vast supplies of gold and silver. He described the great army of warriors ready to do Montezuma's bidding.

Despite this daunting description, Bernal Díaz notes, "Such is the nature of us Spaniards that the more he told us about the fortress and bridges, the more we longed to try our fortune."

# The Tlaxcalan Campaign

Cortés next marched into Tlaxcalan territory. The Tlaxcalans were enemies of Montezuma, and Cortés might have expected a friendlier reception here, but the Tlaxcalans had learned of Cortés's attempts to establish friendly relations with Montezuma's men in previous encounters. They determined to ambush Cortés as soon as he crossed their borders.

It began when two men, traveling ahead of Cortés's entourage and acting as scouts, spotted 15 Indians who quickly retreated. Cortés, learning of this, galloped after them, hoping to capture them and use them to negotiate for peaceful passage through Tlaxcalan territory. Instead the Tlaxcalans turned and fought fiercely. When the skirmish ended, all the Indians had been killed, as well as three of Cortés's cavalrymen and two of the horses. Two more horses were injured.

The skirmish quickly escalated into a much wider battle. Some 3,000 Indians appeared ahead, as the rest of Cortés's army marched up from behind. Both sides soon began fighting, and some 50 Indians were killed before their army retreated.

Cortés and his men camped near a river, and the next day continued their march, only to encounter an army of about 6,000 warriors advancing toward them with drumbeats and loud shouts. Cortés attempted to explain his peaceful intentions but the Indians attacked.

At first the battle went well for Cortés and his men. They were able to kill or wound a significant number of the Indians, who then retreated into the woods or into a nearby canyon. Cortés urged his men forward, intending to quickly bring an end to the battle with a final assault, when a frightening sight caused him to stop.

An army of some 40,000 Tlaxcalan warriors appeared in rows above and around them, stretching far into the distance. They were naked, painted in red and white, and many were chanting or shouting.

Cortés was forced to quickly assess the situation while calming his men. The ground was rough and uneven, making it difficult for the horses to move forward. Cortés ordered his men into a tight formation—a kind of extended square—as the Indians advanced with a hail of arrows and stones. The Spaniards had only one clear advantage: Their weapons were superior, and as they began hand-to-hand combat they were able to inflict some damage with their swords and rifles. Eventually they were able to maneuver the cannons into position, inflicting even greater damage.

Still the great Tlaxcalan army continued in wave after wave. When one group was pushed back, another appeared. The Spaniards dared not break ranks; those that did were immediately wounded. They continued to slowly push forward, a square of some 300 men fighting on all four sides. Finally, as the day came to a close, the Tlaxcalans retreated. It was September 2, 1519, and the Spaniards had survived their first serious battle.

Cortés quickly assessed the situation as the men rested in a hilltop overlook. One of his cavalrymen (and his horse) had been killed. Many had been badly wounded. Cortés was relieved that so few of his men had been killed but, as Buddy Levy notes in *Conquistador*, this was due to the battle tactics of the Tlaxcalans (and later the Aztecs). They believed it more honorable to capture live prisoners for sacrifice than to kill enemies in battle. Warriors who captured leaders or chiefs alive and then presented them for sacrifice were awarded the highest honors.

A day passed, and once more the Tlaxcalan army attacked them. Again, Cortés's use of formations and superior weaponry kept the Spaniards safely entrenched in their position. Only one Spaniard lost his life. Cortés ordered that he be buried deep under a house so that the Tlaxcalans would not realize a life had been lost. Cortés hoped to convey the message that he and his men could not be killed.

The Tlaxcalans were confused about their inability to defeat the Spaniards. There had been rumors that the Spaniards were gods. This they could not believe, but they did begin to suspect that the Spaniards (like their gods) obtained their pow-

## AZTEC RELIGIOUS BELIEFS

The Aztec people placed great importance on their relationship with their gods. There were festivals, feasts, and celebrations throughout the year that marked this relationship. The Aztecs looked to their gods for rain, for food, for life itself. They believed that their gods required offerings in order to be appeased into giving them rain, or victory in a battle, or even for making the sun rise each day. These offerings might be incense, flowers, or small animals, but the Aztec belief was that the greatest sacrifice they could offer was a human, particularly human blood and hearts.

This custom was horrifying to Cortés and his men—it is horrifying to modern readers as well—but in the Aztec belief the gods received nourishment from these offerings. So the sacrifice of a valiant warrior—perhaps a brave enemy captured in battle—was considered the greatest offering that could be made.

The Aztecs worshipped approximately 1,600 different gods, each of which controlled a different aspect of daily life. One of the chief gods was Huitzilopochtli, who was believed to be the god of the sun, of war, and of sacrifice. There were other gods of creation and death, of rain, of harvests, and of commerce. There were patron gods for goldsmiths, merchants, hunters, and kings. There was even a god of gambling, to whom prayers were offered before participating in certain sports and games.

Most Aztec homes were simple structures, but all contained a shrine to a particular god or gods. There were idols both at these home shrines and in the larger temples to represent the gods.

er from the sun. Perhaps if they attacked at night, the Spaniards could be defeated.

Cortés had ordered his men to dress for battle even in their sleep and to keep their weapons close at hand. When guards noticed suspicious movements nearby one night, Cortés and his men were ready. As the Tlaxcalans moved into open ground, Cortés ordered his cannons to fire. The horses were used to add to an atmosphere of fear, as they charged toward the Tlaxcalans in the darkness. Many of the Tlaxcalans were wounded, and about 20 were killed. The Spaniards did not lose a man.

## Message from Montezuma

Word of these victories quickly spread, traveling throughout the land and on to Montezuma. The Tlaxcalans were one of the groups that Montezuma had never been able to conquer. Their fierceness and vast army had made it impossible. Yet, somehow Cortés and his men had not been defeated.

Soon six Aztecs appeared at Cortés's camp. They brought gifts from Montezuma, including gold. They also brought an offer: Montezuma would agree to become a servant of Spain, paying annual sums to its king in gold, slaves, women, and jade. In exchange, Cortés and his men must go home, abandoning their planned journey to Tenochtitlán.

Cortés accepted the gifts and politely explained that he had specific instructions from his king. He had been told to visit Montezuma personally, and he must obey. Once more he asked for a meeting with the Aztec ruler.

Within a few days, some 50 Tlaxcalans appeared at the Spanish camp, carrying gifts of food: cakes of maize, figs and cherries, and roasted turkeys. The men ate ravenously. But Doña Marina hurried to Cortés and warned him that the Tlaxcalans distributing the food were actually spies, who were scouting out the camp and observing the condition of the men and horses. They were also determining the numbers in each hut and the best ways in and out. Cortés seized 17 of the Tlaxcalans, and cut off their hands or their thumbs. He then sent them back with a message: Make peace or else.

The next day, the leader of the Tlaxcalan army, Xicotenga, rode into the camp surrounded by other chiefs from the nearby towns. They brought gifts and apologized for attacking Cortés and his men. They had incorrectly believed them to be allies of their enemies, the Aztecs. They complimented Cortés on his military skills and said that they were now ready to negotiate for peace.

They expressed their willingness to become the servants of Cortés and his king. Xicotenga invited Cortés and his men to come into the city, where they would be welcomed. But lastly, and most significantly, they offered to accompany Cortés and his army, should he choose to fight against Montezuma.

The Tlaxcalan campaign had tested Cortés and his men, but they had survived. More importantly, they had gained a large stretch of territory, and an army of thousands—an army powerful enough to meet the forces of Montezuma.

## Critical Information

On September 23, 1519, Cortés and his men made the 30-mile journey into Tlaxcala as the guest of Xicotenga. The path into the city was lined by Indians, who had placed flowers along the road. Cortés spent three weeks here, resting and feasting, although the wary Cortés continually urged his men to be ready for an attack.

Xicotenga and many of the other chiefs provided Cortés with valuable information during their stay. The Tlaxcalans knew much about the Aztec capital, including the number of drawbridges into the city and the depth of the lake. Having fought (and defeated) the Aztecs on several occasions, their information about the army was particularly important. They emphasized that Montezuma's army in Tenochtitlán alone numbered some 150,000 men. They described the Aztec methods of war and the weapons they used.

Xicotenga offered an army of 100,000 men to go with Cortés. Cortés declined this offer, asking for only 6,000 this time. Then he prepared for departure.

He headed toward Cholula, rather than due west, directly toward Tenochtitlán. A group of ambassadors had come from Montezuma, urging him to go first to Cholula. The people were friendly and he would be treated well while he waited for Montezuma to decide whether or not to meet him. The ambassadors offered to serve as his guides. Despite warnings from the Tlaxcalans that the Aztecs could not be trusted, Cortés accepted the offer. His goal was the city of Quetzalcoatl.

After a day of marching, a group of Indians from Cholula arrived, bringing food and the traditional burning incense. They explained that they wanted to welcome Cortés and his men to Cholula, but that he must leave the Tlaxcalans, their sworn enemies, behind. Cortés agreed, instructing the Tlaxcalan force to wait outside the city limits.

The temple of Quetzalcoatl rose high over the city as Cortés and his men entered. It was an amazing structure, reached by 120 steps and a site where hundreds of thousands of pilgrims came each year to worship the god Quetzalcoatl. The city of Cholula had been inhabited for more than 1,000 years when Cortés and his men first entered the city. Thousands of people lived here; the city was known for its production of fine jewelry and textiles. There were freshwater wells scattered about, and the streets were clean and neat.

As the Spaniards were resting, an envoy sent by Montezuma arrived in the city. With them were several of Montezuma's fiercest warriors. They met with the leaders of Cholula and made arrangements with them to ambush Cortés and his men. Montezuma had determined that Cortés's defeat of the Tlaxcalans marked a dangerous beginning of what could be a fatal trend for the Aztec Empire. Other tribes might be persuaded to join the Spaniards. Revolt could not be tolerated.

## Failed Plot

Cortés began to grow suspicious when, on the fourth day, visits from local chiefs ended, as did the food brought to the Spaniards. Doña Marina had been invited into the home of a Cholulan leader, whose wife she had befriended. The wife warned Doña Marina that she should not return to Cortés's camp. Her husband, as well as other soldiers in the Cholulan army, were planning to attack the Spaniards when they left Cholula for Tenochtitlán.

Thinking quickly, Doña Marina told the woman that she needed to return to the Spanish camp to get some of her belongings. She then hurried to Cortés and told him what she had learned.

Cortés summoned the Cholulan leaders, thanked them for their hospitality, and told them that he and his men would begin their preparations for departure. Then, while the Spanish soldiers began to pack up their equipment and belongings, Cortés gathered a few of his most trusted men and laid out a plot designed to carry a stark message throughout the region.

He asked that the people of Cholula gather at the large central courtyard, near the temple of Quetzalcoatl, so that he could say his final good-byes. Armed Spanish guards stood nearby as the people assembled in the courtyard. As they were gathering, Cortés asked if the caciques of the town might come to his private quarters for one last meeting. Once they had arrived, Cortés blocked the doors and confronted them, telling them that he had learned of their plot and that his king's laws dictated that such treachery must be punished.

At Cortés's signal a gun was fired—the cue for a horrible massacre to begin. Spanish soldiers blocked the exits of the courtyard and began firing their weapons and using their swords on the people, most of whom were unarmed. The leaders trapped in Cortés's quarters were also executed. Next, the Spaniards allowed the Tlaxcalans who had been barred from the city to enter. Both Spaniards and Tlaxcalans roamed the streets, looting homes and killing everyone they met. Some 5,000 people died during the massacre.

At last, Cortés ordered the corpses removed and the streets cleaned. A few priests appeared and were told that they were now safe and to send for any of the people who might have escaped to the hills. The envoys sent by Montezuma had been in hiding during the massacre. When they finally emerged, Cortés told them that the Cholulans had accused the Aztecs of plotting the ambush but he knew that Montezuma was his friend and would never have allowed such treachery. He told them that he planned to continue his march to Tenochtitlán, where he hoped that Montezuma would meet with him.

Messengers hurried back to Montezuma with horrific tales of the massacre at Cholula. It seemed impossible that the Spaniards had, yet again, survived an attack on them. Some of the people were now convinced that Cortés and his men were gods. Montezuma spent several days in prayer and meditation before finally dispatching more messengers to Cortés. They brought food, finely crafted items of clothing, and 10 plates of solid gold. They also brought word that Montezuma had, at last, invited Cortés to meet with him in Tenochtitlán.

## Tenochtitlán

Bernal Díaz, in his account of the Spaniards' first sighting of the region surrounding the Aztec capital, offers a glimpse of the wonder of these men at the beauty of what they encountered:

> When we saw all those cities and villages built in the water, and other great towns on dry land, and that straight

and level causeway leading to Mexico, we were astounded. These great towns . . . and buildings rising from the water, all made of stone, seemed like an enchanted vision. . . . Indeed, some of our soldiers asked whether it was not all a dream. . . . It was all so wonderful that I do not know how to describe this first glimpse of things never heard of, seen or dreamed of before.

The Spaniards were housed in spacious palaces, built of stone, cedar wood, or the wood of other sweet-smelling trees. There were large rooms and outdoor courtyards draped in awnings of woven cotton. There were orchards and gardens, full of brilliantly colored flowers, fragrant rose bushes and fruit trees, and exotic birds. The gardens were built over the water, and canoes floated in and out. The structures had been scrubbed with lime so that they gleamed a bright white.

Cortés and his men reached the gates of Tenochtitlán on November 8, 1519, some nine months after they had left Cuba in search of new settlements for Spain. Cortés and his men, many on horseback and clad in their armor, were escorted by Montezuma's welcoming committee through the gates and over the drawbridge. They then waited for the arrival of Montezuma.

Thousands of people had gathered to watch the sight of the strange Spaniards and their horses riding into Tenochtitlán. Cortés had arrived at last at what many experts say was the most populated city in the world. According to Buddy Levy in *Conquistador*, the population of Europe's largest city at the time—Paris—was between 100,000 and 150,000. The population of Tenochtitlán alone is estimated to have been between 200,000 and 300,000—its entire metropolitan area contained between 1 million and 2.6 million people.

Montezuma arrived at last, carried on an elaborate litter (couch) decorated with gold, silver, and pearls. There was a canopy over his head of rich green feathers. Montezuma

Several times, Cortés requested a meeting with Montezuma. Although Montezuma thought Cortés was an emissary of the serpent god and he provided the Spanish with lavish gifts, Montezuma still refused to meet with Cortés. After the explorers survived several attacks, Montezuma considered them untouchable and finally agreed to meet (*depicted above*).

himself was dressed in magnificent robes, and wore jewel-studded sandals with golden soles. As he stepped down, members of his entourage hurried forward to sweep the ground and then place their cloaks upon it before he walked forward.

Cortés dismounted from his horse, and the two men bowed to each other. Montezuma presented Cortés with two beautiful golden necklaces, and then told him that he must be tired from his journey. He instructed his attendants to usher Cortés and his men to their quarters, where they were given elaborate accommodations. Even the horses were given beds of flowers to sleep on. Cortés then stepped forward, intending to embrace Montezuma, but several of Montezuma's princes grasped Cortés to prevent him from touching their leader.

After a fine meal, Cortés was invited to meet with Montezuma. He took with him a few chosen men, as well as Doña Marina to translate. Montezuma seated Cortés on a throne next to his own, and presented him with an array of gifts, including fine clothing and textiles, elaborate examples of finely crafted featherwork, gold, and silver.

Montezuma then made an elaborate speech, welcoming Cortés and noting that his coming had been foretold in prophecy and in Montezuma's own dreams. Controversy surrounds precisely what Montezuma said and how it should be interpreted. In the speech, Montezuma alluded to Cortés's relationship to the Aztec gods, describing the city as "his" (Cortés's) city. This no doubt was meant as an allegory, but Cortés undoubtedly seized upon the phrases and would use them to justify his later actions.

Montezuma then invited Cortés and his men to relax and wander the city. He gave them guides and ordered servants to provide them with food and anything else they needed.

The next day, Montezuma again invited Cortés to his palace. After giving him a tour of the rooms and halls—there were more than 100 in total, with painted walls and ceilings and workshops where the most skilled artisans created jewelry, pottery, and featherwork—Montezuma invited Cortés back to his throne room.

Cortés had invited a few trusted men to accompany him. In addition to Doña Marina, Bernal Díaz was there. In his memoir, Díaz describes what happened next:

> Then he [Cortés] very carefully expounded the creation of the world, how we are all brothers, the children of one mother and father called Adam and Eve; and how such a brother as our great Emperor . . . had sent us to tell him this, so that he might put a stop to it, and so that they might give up the worship of idols and make no more human sacrifices—for all men are brothers. . . . He also promised that in the course of time the King would send some men who lead holy lives among us, much better than our own, to explain this more fully, for we had only come to give them warning.

After the hospitality he had shown Cortés, Montezuma must have been offended at this assault on his religious beliefs. Nonetheless, he replied carefully that he had already learned of Cortés's religious beliefs. Díaz writes that Montezuma then added, "We have worshipped our own gods here from the beginning and know them to be good. No doubt yours are good also, but do not trouble to tell us any more about them at present."

For the next week, Cortés and his men moved through Tenochtitlán. Montezuma (who Díaz estimated to be about 40 years old) lived in the largest palace, guarded by about 3,000 armed warriors and serviced by more than 1,000 servants. Díaz noted that at each meal Montezuma was offered more than 30 dishes, kept warm on small earthenware cookers before they were served. His servants never looked him in the face. Instead, as they approached, they bowed three times. He ate his meals behind a screen crafted from wood and decorated with gold so that no one would see him eat. He drank many cups of cocoa each day, served in cups made of pure gold.

The palace also contained a zoo, with jaguars, mountain lions, wolves, snakes, crocodiles, and birds of many varieties. There were vast gardens containing roses of different colors, as well as herbs used for healing.

In the center of town was a marketplace, where more than 60,000 people came to trade and buy goods every five days. There were stalls for pottery, for textiles, for building materials, for jewels. You could buy salt, cotton, tobacco, chocolate, and food of all kinds. You could buy slaves at one booth, children's toys at another.

The Spaniards, as they roamed the city, saw a sporting arena, where a game called *tlachtli* was played. This game involved putting a rubber ball through two large stone hoops using only the elbows or hips. Participants wore leather pads on their chins, knees, elbows, and shoulders and performed to large crowds of wealthy citizens.

There were large temples, too, sacred places that were forbidden to the Spaniards. Cortés asked Montezuma for permission to visit the Great Temple of Huitzilopochtli, the god of war, and Montezuma's own personal place of worship. It was a sacred place, but Montezuma finally agreed to escort Cortés himself to the large pyramid. The place of worship was reached by climbing 114 steep stone steps. When he reached the flat top, Cortés had a sweeping view of Tenochtitlán, stretching out for miles below him.

The shrine to Huitzilopochtli at the top bore the bloodstains of countless victims of sacrifice. Inside the inner shrine, there were several small braziers, or containers, used for heating incense and other items. Inside these, according to Díaz, the Aztec priests were "burning the hearts of three Indians whom they had sacrificed that day; and all the walls of that shrine were so splashed and caked with blood that they and the floor too were black. Indeed, the whole place stank abominably."

Díaz notes that Cortés then spoke to Montezuma, stating, "I cannot imagine how a prince as great and wise as your Majesty can have failed to realize that these idols of yours are not gods but evil things, the proper name for which is devils." He then asked Montezuma for permission to put a cross at the top of the temple.

Montezuma and his attendants were deeply insulted at Cortés's comments. As Buddy Levy notes in *Conquistador*, human sacrifice was the ultimate offering in the Aztec belief system, and the idols were critically important to their religious celebrations and forms of worship. According to Díaz, Montezuma replied that he would never have shown Cortés this holy shrine if he had known that he was going to insult his gods. "We hold them to be very good. They give us health and rain and crops and weather, and all the victories we desire," he said. He then told Cortés firmly to say no more about them, and instructed his attendants to lead Cortés and his men away.

Montezuma remained behind at the shrine. He needed to pray to his gods, asking them for forgiveness for the insults of Cortés.

# Battle for Tenochtitlán

THE BATTLE FOR MEXICO BEGAN NOT IN TENOCHTITLÁN BUT in Vera Cruz, the Spanish fortress Cortés had established. The captain Cortés had left in charge—Juan de Escalante—had been murdered with six other Spanish soldiers and several Totonacs. Messengers brought Cortés the news and also the details of who was responsible. Cualpopoca, one of Montezuma's governors, angry that the Spaniards had encouraged the Indians to pay tribute to the Spanish king rather than to Montezuma, had attacked Vera Cruz.

It had been one week since Cortés had arrived in Tenochtitlán. Now he was determined to arrest Montezuma and seize the city for his own. The attack at Vera Cruz provided the perfect excuse.

On November 14, Cortés arranged a meeting with Montezuma. He took 30 armed soldiers with him, as well as six of his officers and Doña Marina. Cortés and his men customarily strolled through the city while armed. The sight of the armed soldiers did not raise any alarms when they arrived at Montezuma's palace.

Cortés told Montezuma what had happened at Vera Cruz. He then said that he was concerned that Montezuma might be planning to trap him and his men at Tenochtitlán.

Bernal Díaz recounted in his memoirs what happened next:

> I have no desire to start a war on this account, or to destroy this city, Cortés said. Everything will be forgiven, provided you will now come quietly with us to our quarters, and make no protest. You will be as well served and attended there as in your own palace. But if you cry out, or raise any commotion, you will immediately be killed by these captains of mine, whom I have brought for this purpose.

Montezuma was shocked and protested his innocence in the attack at Vera Cruz. He said that he would not leave his palace against his will. After Cortés's captains emphasized their intention either to take him prisoner or kill him, Montezuma reluctantly agreed to go. Cortés instructed him to make it clear to his guards that he wanted to stay with the Spaniards for a while, and that he was leaving of his own free will.

It is hard to understand why Montezuma did not simply call out to his guards for help. Cortés and his men might have been able to hold out for a while, but 30 men could not have defeated all of Montezuma's household and army.

Hammond Innes in *The Conquistadors* suggests that Montezuma was simply not accustomed to anyone defying him and threatening violence. He had been king for 18 years, and his authority over religious and political life was absolute. No one questioned him directly. No one even dared to look him in the face.

In addition, Montezuma was susceptible to the rumors that suggested Cortés might be a god. Perhaps his victory was the will of the gods. Montezuma decided to obey.

## The Prisoner King

Cortés gave specific instructions that Montezuma was to be treated courteously. He was allowed to go to his temple to worship, though accompanied by armed Spanish guards. He continued to receive guests, to hold meetings and go about much of the business of his court, but it was clear that he was no longer a free man. Soon, word of the capture of the king spread throughout the kingdom.

While in custody, Montezuma sent for Cualpopoca, the governor responsible for the attack at Vera Cruz. Montezuma was convinced that Cualpopoca would be able to testify to his innocence in the matter, and that then Cortés would release him.

When Cualpopoca arrived 20 days later, Montezuma told Cortés to question him about the events at Vera Cruz. Cortés took Cualpopoca, his son, and the 15 men who had come with him and put them in chains. According to Cortés's secretary, Francisco López de Gómara, "they were more severely questioned," meaning that they were tortured. They ultimately confessed that they had killed the Spaniards under orders from Montezuma, and Cortés swiftly sentenced them to be burned alive at the stake and placed in the central square clearly visible from the rooms where Montezuma was being held.

Gómara describes the impact on the many people who had gathered to witness this execution: "The people . . . looked on in complete silence, without rioting, terrified by this novel form of justice imposed in the kingdom of Montezuma, by strangers and guests of their great lord."

For the next five months, Montezuma remained Cortés's prisoner. Montezuma held meetings, attempting to convince his noblemen that he was still in charge, but no one was fooled.

Meanwhile, Cortés began to formulate plans for cementing his control over Tenochtitlán. Boats, he believed, would help in this effort, and also give him an escape route if necessary. He selected one of his soldiers to oversee their construction. He also sent to Vera Cruz for some of the spare boat parts—the compasses, ropes, sails, and oars—that had been rescued from his previous fleet before it was sunk. The boats were designed so that they could either be sailed or rowed with oars. They would be constructed to carry up to 75 soldiers, as well as horses and cannons.

After four had been constructed, Cortés sailed on them several times, making careful note of the lake regions around the city. He studied their depth, the effect of differing wind directions, and the layout of the water.

Cortés also began pressuring Montezuma to reveal the source of the gold that seemed to flow through the kingdom. Montezuma and his people valued jade and featherwork far more than gold. The Spaniards' obsession with it was often amusing to them. Montezuma willingly told him the areas where gold was mined, and Cortés organized three expeditions to these mining regions.

He also pressured Montezuma to make formal the fact that the kingdom now belonged to King Charles V of Spain. Reluctantly, Montezuma called a meeting of his noblemen and spoke of the prophecy that suggested that gods would come from a distant land to rule over them. Cortés and the Spaniards fulfilled this prophecy. He instructed his noblemen to now pay tributes to the Spanish king and his representative—Cortés—as they had once paid tribute to him. Montezuma was crying as he spoke these words, and his noblemen, too, were in tears. Nonetheless, they decided to obey their king. Gold, silver, and jewels were swiftly seized. Much of the beautifully crafted gold was melted down to be reshaped into bars for easier measuring.

At last, it was the treasure the Spaniards had dreamed of and fought for. But after Cortés had ensured that one-fifth of the treasure was set aside for King Charles V, he postponed dividing it amongst the men. Bernal Díaz notes in his memoirs

Cortés used the attack on the Spanish in Vera Cruz by Montezuma's governer, Cualpopoca, as the perfect excuse to arrest Montezuma and seize Tenochtitlán. Montezuma and his men were required to swear allegiance to King Charles V of Spain. In this painting, Montezuma submits himself as a subject of the Spanish king before Cortés.

that "when the pieces taken from Montezuma's treasury were broken up there had been much more gold in the piles, and that a third of it was now missing." His suggestion is that Cortés had hidden much of it away for himself. In the end, Cortés insisted that he, too, must receive a fifth of all the wealth that was seized. Then the wages must be paid out for all of the professional sailors and the priests. The men who remained in Vera Cruz also deserved a share. By the time all these debts were accounted for, each man received a very small share of the vast wealth.

Gold was only one part of the mission in Cortés's mind. He also wanted to convert the people of Montezuma's kingdom to the Christian faith. He took a group of soldiers to the Great Temple, climbed to the top, and confronted the priests, explaining his intention to destroy their idols and replace them with statues of Jesus and the Virgin Mary. The Aztec priests laughed at him, convinced that their gods would destroy any man who dared touch the idols.

Cortés strode over to the huge idols and began striking at them. Montezuma, learning of this, hurried to the temple. Rather than destroying the idols, he argued, why not simply make room for more? Cortés agreed, provided that no more human sacrifices were permitted. An agreement was reached, a Catholic church was built at the top of the pyramid, and Mass was said there.

Rumors of rebellion were sweeping through the city after this latest act by Cortés and his men. Doña Marina warned Cortés that she was hearing talk that an attack against the Spaniards could happen at any moment.

And then, in a meeting with Montezuma, Cortés learned of something even more troubling. Montezuma told him that his messengers had brought news of a fleet of ships that had arrived off the coast of Vera Cruz. He showed Cortés the sketches his messengers had brought—pictures of 19 ships, as well as many men and horses. He told Cortés that these ships would provide him with a way to leave and return to his home. He did not tell Cortés that he had already made contact with these new arrivals.

Cortés studied the sketches, considered the numbers, and knew that such a large fleet had not come from Spain. It had come from Jamaica or Cuba. Someone was trying to rob him not only of the wealth he had found, but of his right to govern this new land.

## Struggle for New Spain

Cortés's suspicions were correct. The fleet had come from Cuba, dispatched by Diego Velázquez. Velázquez had learned of the founding of Vera Cruz, of Cortés's claim to be captain-general of the new settlement, of the gold he had sent to the Spanish king, and of his plans to conquer the entire country.

Velázquez had decided that Cortés either needed to be captured or killed. Then all of New Spain would be his. He chose his friend Pánfilo de Narváez to lead the expedition. Narváez had been at the head of the expedition that had conquered Cuba, with Cortés serving under him. Now he was leading a fleet with more than 800 men, more than double the size of Cortés's force, with 20 cannons and more than four times as many horses. They had set out for Vera Cruz on March 5, 1520.

Narváez did not immediately attack Vera Cruz. Instead, he decided to try diplomacy, and sent three men to demand the surrender of the settlement. Captain Gonzalo de Sandoval, who had been placed in charge after the death of Escalante, quickly arrested the three men and sent them to Tenochtitlán, along with a letter telling Cortés of the danger Vera Cruz was facing.

Cortés had already decided to organize a force to go to the aid of Vera Cruz when the letter arrived, along with Narváez's three envoys. Cortés wisely treated the three men with great courtesy, offering them luxurious accommodations, preparing a feast, and displaying some of the great treasure that had been seized in Tenochtitlán. He then gave them numerous gifts and sent them back to Narváez.

Cortés suspected that the sight of the gold and the tales of the splendors of Tenochtitlán might inspire more than a few of Narváez's men to desert and join Cortés. He was correct. He was further helped by a letter Narváez sent to Cortés, explaining his intention to seize the treasure that had been won and arrest his traitorous crew. Cortés read this letter out loud to his men, ensuring that they knew their only chance at a fortune lay with Cortés.

Cortés then led a force of 250 men to the coast, placing Pedro de Alvarado in command of the remaining force at Tenochtitlán and in charge of Montezuma. Around May 28, he reached the area where Narváez and his remaining men were camped.

Narváez had a clear advantage in numbers, but his men had not yet faced a battle. Cortés's force was accustomed to fighting and to the conditions in Mexico. They crept up in the night, in the midst of a heavy rain. Within an hour, Narváez had been captured and his men surrendered. The men joined Cortés; Narváez was sent in chains to Vera Cruz, where he was imprisoned for several years.

Cortés now had a far larger fighting force and he divided them, some to be stationed at Vera Cruz, while others marched back with him to Tenochtitlán. They needed to move quickly, for Cortés had received terrible news from Pedro de Alvarado. The Aztecs had attacked. Alvarado and his men could not hold out much longer.

## Battle for Mexico

Soon after Cortés's departure from Tenochtitlán, Alvarado had noticed a change in the city. He had only 120 men, and Montezuma spent lengthy times in whispered discussions with members of his court. Then the Aztecs stopped bringing food to the Spaniards.

During their time in Mexico, the soldiers had learned that when food was no longer brought battle soon followed. Alvarado was also nervous that he had heard nothing from Cortés. He knew that Montezuma and Narváez had exchanged messages, and worried that Narváez might already have defeated Cortés and be on his way to the city.

The Aztecs had been given permission to celebrate their Festival of Toxcatl, an annual celebration that involved dancing, music, and sacrifice in a ceremony intended to bring the rains that watered their crops and made life possible. The courtyard filled with the Aztec aristocracy, and several thousand of their warriors, as well as 500 dancers and many drummers and flutists. As the music began, the nervous Spaniards, believing that they would soon be sacrificed, suddenly attacked, massacring the unarmed Aztecs.

When word of the brutal murder of their leaders and warriors reached the people, they rushed to the palace to recover their dead and revenge them. The Spanish had an advantage in firepower and, using cannons, rifles, and arrows, they were temporarily able to keep the Aztecs at bay. But their weapons would not last forever, and more and more Aztecs were rushing into the capital. Worse, they had burned the four ships Cortés had built. Now there was no means of escape, and the Spaniards had neither food nor water.

Cortés hurried back along the route he had so recently traveled, a distance of some 250 miles. On June 24, 1520, he crossed back into Tenochtitlán and prepared for trouble, but the streets were practically deserted. It was eerily quiet, a city in mourning.

They headed for the palace, where they were welcomed by the emaciated and dehydrated Spaniards. Cortés was furious with Alvarado for attacking with such violence when he had been able to hold the city for six months without any blood being shed. He was also furious with Montezuma, refusing to meet with him and instead sending one of his men to order Montezuma to have the markets opened and life to resume as normal. Montezuma sadly replied that no one would listen to him any longer. Instead, he suggested sending his brother, Cuitláhuac.

Cuitláhuac was released and immediately assembled the surviving noblemen and warriors. He told them that Montezuma was no longer capable of ruling the Aztecs. The noblemen swiftly decided that Montezuma was no longer king of the Aztecs. The new ruler was Cuitláhuac.

Cuitláhuac then led an attack against the Spaniards. Using arrows and javelins, throwing rocks and spears, the Aztecs were able to breach the walls where Cortés and his men were fortified. They shot flaming arrows into the structure, setting the palace on fire in several places. There was no water. The fires had to be put out by smothering them. Many of the Spaniards were wounded or killed. Cortés himself was injured when an Aztec clubbed him.

Cortés ordered his men out to the roof to shoot their cannons and rifles. Hundreds of Aztecs were killed in the street below.

For nearly a week, the battle continued. The Aztecs would launch an attack against the Spaniards, who would fight them off with superior firepower. The Spaniards were running low on food, water, and gunpowder. They would not be able to last forever.

## Montezuma's Final Words

In desperation, Cortés ordered Montezuma to go out on the roof and speak to his people to see if he could persuade them to end the attack. He refused, according to Bernal Díaz, saying, "I do not believe that I can do anything towards ending this war, because they have already chosen another lord, and made up their minds not to let you leave this place alive. I believe therefore that all of you will be killed."

Cortés decided to force Montezuma to the roof. Several of his soldiers led the former king up to the edge of the roof, hoping that the people would see him and allow him to speak. Instead, a shower of stones and arrows fell all around him.

The Aztecs engaged in several battles with the Spanish and Cortés. After a week of fighting, the Spanish were running low on food, firepower, and soldiers. In a last-ditch effort, Cortés pushed Montezuma onto the roof of his palace to plead with the Aztecs to surrender. Montezuma was wounded in a shower of arrows and stones by his own men and died three days later.

Montezuma was struck in the head and chest. He survived for a few days, but then died on June 30, 1520.

Cortés no longer had Montezuma to use as a hostage. The army he was fighting had the advantage in numbers, and the Spaniards desperately needed supplies. As Cortés looked out over the city, he could see that, one by one, the bridges into Tenochtitlán were being destroyed by the Aztecs. They hoped to prevent the Spaniards from escaping or reinforcements from coming to their aid.

Finally, only one bridge remained, and Cortés decided that he and his men must somehow get across it and on to the safety of the mainland. They decided to escape at night, since the Aztecs had proved less skillful at fighting in the dark.

It would not be possible to take the full supply of Montezuma's treasure. According to *Conquistador*, the total of gold, silver, and gemstones weighed eight tons. Cortés secured first the king's fifth and his own fifth and selected his most trustworthy guards to protect it. It would be carried out by eight Tlaxcalans and a few of the remaining horses. Cortés then told his men that they could take whatever they could carry, warning them that they would also need to be prepared to fight and so should not overburden themselves. Bernal Díaz writes that his own focus was on saving his life rather than weighing himself down with treasure. He took four jewels and hid them under his armor. He would later use them to buy himself food and medicine for his wounds. Some of the men were less cautious, particularly those who had served under Narváez. They loaded pockets and bags with gold and silver.

Shortly after midnight on July 1, 1520, Cortés and his men slipped out of the palace and made their way through the streets of Tenochtitlán. It was foggy, and a heavy rain had begun. For a while, the sound of the rain masked the noise of Cortés's departure. But just as they reached the bridge, a woman spotted them and called out. Within minutes, the sound of drumbeats could be heard and Aztec soldiers hurried from all sides.

The bridge was the shortest leading into Tenochtitlán. While some Spaniards made it across, others were still trapped on the bridge when the fighting began. Aztecs launched canoes and paddled furiously across the water, chasing those who had already crossed. It was impossible for the Spaniards to close into any kind of formation. Instead, in a panic, they ran for their lives. Bernal Díaz writes, "The channel, or water-gap, was soon filled up with dead horses, Indians of both sexes, servants, bundles, and boxes. . . . Those of us who escaped only did so by the grace of God."

There were many who did not escape. Both Aztecs and Spaniards were killed and wounded in the furious fighting, and the dark added to the confusion and fear. Most of Narváez's men slipped into the water and drowned or were captured and taken away to be sacrificed, weighed down by the gold they had carried out of the city. The Spaniards would refer to that night as La Noche Triste—The Night of Sorrows—to describe the day on which nearly 600 of their men were killed, as well as some 4,000 Tlaxcalans. They also lost most of their gunpowder, all of their cannons, and both the king's fifth and Cortés's fifth, all of which had slipped into the water in the frenzy of battle.

Cortés's secretary, Gómara, records the commander's reaction when he learned of all that had been lost:

> At this point Cortés stopped and even sat down, not to rest, but to mourn over the dead and those still living, and to consider the heavy blow that fate had dealt him in the loss of so many friends, such treasures, such authority, and such a great city and kingdom. Not only did he bemoan his present misfortune, but feared those to come, because all his men were wounded and he knew not what way to turn.

Cortés was fortunate that the Aztecs did not pursue him. Instead, as dawn broke, they stopped to carry away their dead, sacrifice those who had been captured, and celebrate their victory. Had they chased the Spaniards and engaged them again in battle, the Spaniards would not have survived.

## Battle at Otumba

Cortés and his men made their way north for a week, fighting small battles with roaming parties of Aztecs they encountered. They were exhausted, marching while wounded and finding only bits of maize and herbs to eat. Finally, they reached the valley outside the city of Otumba, where they planned to camp and rest.

Spanish scouts, sent out to survey the surrounding area, came back with frightening news: A massive Aztec army had gathered a short distance away. Cortés followed the scouts and saw, in Gómara's words, "a multitude that covered the country and surrounded them." The valley was full of warriors carrying shields and spears, wearing helmets with bright green feathers.

The Spaniards had no gunpowder left, so they would need to rely on their cavalrymen. The soldiers were equipped with pikes, swords, and lances. Most of them believed that they would not survive this battle. Cortés encouraged the men, instructing the cavalry, according to Bernal Díaz, to "cut our way through them, and leave none of them without a wound!"

Cortés instructed the men to keep in a defensive rectangle, and not to break formation. They fought for several hours, with both armies swinging and hacking away at each other. The Spaniards faced certain extinction until Cortés noticed that each time the horses charged at the Aztecs, they created a temporary gap in the Aztec formation. Cortés quickly called out to the men to press forward each time the horses charged, and into the gap they rushed and slashed away at the enemy, using the disorder created by the horses.

Then Cortés spotted the commander of the Aztec army moving beneath his flag, wearing golden armor and high silver plumes. Cortés rushed forward, knocked the commander to the ground, and seized the flag. The flag had served as the direction point for the army, and without its guidance and the instructions of their commander, the Aztecs quickly grew confused and soon were forced into retreat. With that, the battle ended.

Buddy Levy describes the battle of Otumba as one of Cortés's greatest military achievements. Despite seemingly impossible odds (Cortés's secretary, Gómara, writes that the Aztec army numbered 200,000), the Spanish had won by using their horses and strict military formation.

# Final Conquest

Hernán Cortés benefitted from extraordinary good luck in his effort to conquer Mexico, and the most crucial events happened in the weeks after the battle at Otumba. Ships began arriving in the area around Vera Cruz over a period of several weeks—there were ultimately six in all. Two were from Cuba and had been sent by Velázquez. Believing that Narváez must now have seized Cortés and be in control of the settlement, Velázquez had sent ships with reinforcements, including men, weapons, and gunpowder. Three more came from the governor of Jamaica, who intended to settle the territory near the mouth of the Panuco River, north of Vera Cruz. In addition to provisions and more men, these ships also brought horses, weapons, and armor. One final ship arrived from Spain. This one had been sent by Cortés's father and several businessmen who wanted to invest in Cortés's expedition in Mexico. This contained men, gunpowder, muskets, and horses.

One by one each ship was lured into Vera Cruz, where the crew was persuaded (often with the use of a sword) to join Cortés. Cortés then welcomed them with gifts, with food, and with stories of the wealth that awaited them. The arrival of those ships expanded Cortés's army by more than 200 healthy men, bringing the total to nearly 1,300, plus supplies, weapons, and gunpowder. He now was ready to launch another attack on Tenochtitlán. He instructed several of his most skilled carpenters to begin building 13 boats. This time, he planned a sea attack.

While Cortés was expanding his army, the crew was resting and recovering from the recent battles. A devastating development in Mexico made his task much easier. Smallpox had begun to spread throughout the country, leaving countless victims suffering from what was to them an unknown illness that had never before existed in the New World. Victims suffered from coughs and were covered with terrible blistering sores before dying.

The illness had come to Mexico on one of Narváez's ships, sent to capture Cortés. On board was an African porter named Francisco de Eguia, who was infected with the illness. It spread from him to the Indians and throughout the country. In Tenochtitlán, the population was devastated by the epidemic. A food shortage followed, since the people were too ill to harvest or prepare the food. For 70 days the disease ravaged the entire countryside. While it is impossible to know precisely how many Aztecs were stricken with the disease, many estimates suggest that more than half the population died. In Tenochtitlán, the new king, Cuitláhuac, was one of the many victims.

Because smallpox had existed in Europe for some time, most of the Spaniards had already been exposed to the illness, so they were not affected. This added to the rumors that the Spaniards must be gods—how else could they remain immune to an illness that killed so many others?

## Final Attack

By December 1520, Cortés led his newly expanded army on a journey of conquest. Many of the towns and cities had lost significant percentages of their population, including their leaders and warriors. Yet, there still were fierce battles all along the route he had drawn up.

Finally, he prepared for a new attack on Tenochtitlán. He had more than 700 foot soldiers, 3 heavy iron guns, 15 small bronze field pieces, half a ton of gunpowder. He had

Smallpox, lack of food and water, and prolonged battles destroyed the city of Tenochtitlán. More than 240,000 died during the battle. With the capture of Cuauhtémoc, the ruler of Tenochtitlán and Montezuma's nephew, on August 13, 1521, the Aztec Empire came to an end. Cortés claimed it for Spain, became its governor, and renamed it Mexico City.

86 horsemen, 118 crossbowmen and musketeers. And the 13 boats were ready. Cortés sent messengers to the tribes in Tlaxcala, Cholula, and the other territories that had signed treaties of alliance with him. He called upon them to send all their warriors for a great battle. Soon he had more than 75,000 Indian warriors at his command.

Cortés divided his forces into three divisions. One would march around Tenochtitlán from the west, one from the south, and the third—led by Cortés himself—would come by boat.

The battle would last two months. When Cortés and his men eventually neared Tenochtitlán, the Aztecs fought bravely, attacking first by canoes, then defending the bridges, then the streets of the city itself. The city had been devastated by smallpox—there were still many unburied corpses littering the streets. Once Cortés and his men had control of the surrounding areas, supplies of food into the city began to dwindle. The fighting was fierce. Captured Spaniards and their Indian allies would swiftly be sacrificed. Cortés ordered his men to tear down and burn many of the Aztec homes.

The battle finally ended on August 13, 1521. The Aztecs had been forced into a last stand in one corner of the city. Cortés pushed in and more than 15,000 Aztecs died on that day in a final attempt to defend their city.

A small stream of refugees began fleeing Tenochtitlán. Bernal Díaz describes the pitiful sight:

> For three whole days and nights they never ceased streaming out, and all three causeways were crowded with men, women, and children, so thin, sallow, dirty, and stinking that it was pitiful to see them. Once the city was free from them Cortés went out to inspect it. We found the houses full of corpses, and some poor Mexicans still in them who could not move away. . . . The city looked as if it had been ploughed up. The roots of any edible greenery had been dug out, boiled, and eaten, and they had even cooked the

bark of some of the trees. There was no fresh water to be found; all of it was brackish.

## Claiming Victory

The stench from the corpses was so great that Cortés ordered his men to set up camps well outside the city. Each day the Spaniards marched in to begin the work of cleaning Tenochtitlán. Fires burned all day and all night, disposing of the corpses.

Cortés failed to recover the great gold treasure that had been lost when he and his army first fled Tenochtitlán. Attempts to explore the water where it was thought to have slipped away yielded little. Rummaging through the homes that were now abandoned yielded some gold and jewels, but

### WHAT THE AZTECS SAW

More than 240,000 people are estimated to have died during the battle for Tenochtitlán. An anonymous Aztec eyewitness revealed how the terrified people viewed the attack by the Spaniards, taken from the PBS Web site "Conquistadors":

A ball of stone comes out shooting sparks and raining fire. It makes smoke that smells of rotten mud. When the ball of stone hits a tree, the trunk splits into splinters, as if it has exploded from the inside. They cover their heads and bodies with metal. Their swords are metal, their bows are metal, their shields and spears are metal. Their deer carry them on their backs, making them as tall as the roof of a house. . . . We are powerless against him. We are nothing compared to these strangers.

far less than the great treasure of Montezuma the Spaniards had seized. The city that had dazzled Cortés and his men was no more. The Aztec nation, with its history and craftsmanship, had been destroyed.

Cortés faced one last threat: a possible challenge by King Charles V to his right to rule Mexico. But the gold that Cortés had sent back to his king, and the letters detailing his exploits, paid off. On October 15, 1522, he received two letters from his king that stated that Hernán Cortés had been appointed captain-general of New Spain.

In the year that transpired between his conquest of Mexico and his official appointment by the king, Cortés had focused on colonizing areas other than Tenochtitlán. He had begun the reconstruction of that city. He had encouraged the destruction of the Aztec idols and their replacement with Christian symbols. And he had continued his search for gold.

The search for gold had marked much of Cortés's time in New Spain. His men had seen the vast riches of Montezuma's kingdom, but after the fall of Tenochtitlán, the gold seemed to have disappeared. Some of the crew began to suspect that Cortés had stolen the gold.

At the time, Cortés was staying in a palace with whitewashed walls. Bernal Díaz notes that every morning Cortés awoke to find that someone had written accusations on the walls with charcoal and ink, saying things like "he had dealt us a worse defeat than he had given to Mexico, and that we ought to call ourselves not the victors of New Spain but the victims of Hernando Cortés." Another said he had not been "content with a general's share but had taken a king's." Cortés began to hand out shares of the land to some of the men, in part to deal with this hint of rebellion, in part to aid in the settling of the vast territory. He became a kind of feudal lord, overseeing numerous small settlements.

Cortés oversaw the reopening of the mines. Cows, pigs, sheep, and horses were brought in from the Caribbean Islands and bred to increase the livestock. Cortés built himself a palace

## Hernán Cortés's Conquest of Mexico, 1518–1521

One of the most important campaigns during Spain's mission to colonize the Americas was the conquest of the Aztec Empire. With the capture of Cuauhtémoc, the successor and nephew of Montezuma, large portions of mainland Mexico came under the control of Spain and King Charles V. The Aztec Empire was destroyed and Tenochtitlán was renamed Mexico City.

on the site where Montezuma's palace had once stood. Christian churches were constructed around the city. He ordered the manufacture of gunpowder and artillery, the former from sulfur obtained from a volcano, the latter from iron discovered near Taxco.

In July 1522, Cortés's wife, Catalina, arrived in a ship from Cuba. They spent several months together in Cortés's palace until one fateful night when, after a party at Cortés's home, Catalina went up to her room. A few hours later, Catalina was dead. There were marks on her neck that suggested she had been strangled. Catalina's maids accused Cortés of murdering her, but the doctors who examined her after her death found that she had died of natural causes, possibly an attack of asthma or a weak heart. Gossip about the true cause of Catalina's death—and Cortés's suspected role in it—lingered for years.

## Later Years

Cortés sent numerous gifts to his king, including an elaborate model cannon constructed from silver. Hugh Thomas in *Conquest* reports that Cortés called the cannon "the Phoenix" and on it he inscribed:

> *This was born without equal*
> *I am without a second in serving you*
> *You are without equal in the world.*

The sheer number and value of the gifts suggests that Cortés had not been fully honest with his men in disclosing precisely how much of Montezuma's treasure was found. But it had an unfortunate side effect. King Charles V, who desperately needed money because of Spain's costly wars with France, sent some of his representatives to New Spain. He wanted to ensure that Cortés was properly providing him with an accurate fifth of all the wealth of this new colony.

Cortés was unhappy with the arrival of these men. They demanded to see the gold, silver, and jewels that had been recovered and wanted an accounting of all that was happening in the colony. Cortés had also made his fair share of enemies. Gradually word began to reach King Charles that Cortés was cheating him, that Cortés had murdered his wife, that Cortés had murdered a whole host of people.

Cortés finally decided to travel to Spain to meet personally with King Charles, provide him with his version of events, and argue for his right to continue to govern New Spain. He traveled with two ships, loading them with gold, silver, and jewels. He also brought several examples of the exotic life in the colony, including tigers, albatrosses, an armadillo, and an opossum. He brought fans made of elaborate feathers, mirrors crafted from jewels, and delicate hair ornaments. All of it was intended to dazzle the king and prove why Cortés should continue as the king's governor.

He left for Spain in the spring of 1528. When he reached land, his fame had preceded him. The man who had left Spain a penniless 19-year-old dreaming of a fortune in the New World had found it and returned to his homeland a rich and powerful 43-year-old who was welcomed by his king.

Cortés was referred to as the "Gran Conquistador." The king received him graciously but when Cortés asked him to be named governor of Mexico the king refused, perhaps no longer willing to invest too much power in one man. Instead, he named him marquess of the Valley of Oazaca and captain-general of New Spain. He gave him vast estates in New Spain and also knighted him, but Cortés did not use the title.

While in Spain, he married a young noblewoman, Doña Juana de Zúñiga, giving her numerous presents, including five huge emeralds shaped like a rose, a bell, a fish, a trumpet, and a cup. Rumors soon reached Cortés that there was trouble in Mexico. Disappointed in his failure to be appointed governor, he determined to return at once.

He landed back in New Spain on July 15, 1530. He no longer had absolute authority; the Spanish king had appointed representatives to oversee various aspects of his colony. Instead Cortés focused on developing his estates, growing sugar, silk, and cotton, raising cattle and horses. He had three daughters and a son with Doña Juana de Zúñiga (his secretary, Francisco

Gómara, reports that he also had two sons and three daughters with Indian women, including a son with Doña Marina).

Cortés continued his efforts to colonize as much of New Spain as possible. He sent out numerous expeditions, and personally participated in the exploration of Mexico's Pacific Coast and the peninsula of Baja California (now part of Mexico) in 1536. It was Cortés who named this territory "California" after an island described in a novel popular in the early 1500s. He attempted the conquest of Honduras and Guatemala, but these expeditions did not succeed.

He also made plans to explore the South Seas, part of his effort to find a shortcut to China. Conflicts over whether or not Cortés had the right to explore these new territories prompted him to make another trip to Spain, in the spring of 1540.

Cortés never returned to Mexico. He spent his final years in Spain waging constant legal battles to win the right to continue his conquests. By now, he was no longer the famous conquistador. The king became tired of his constant requests for recognition.

At last, Cortés settled in Seville, making occasional trips to the court to meet with the king and dreaming of a return to Mexico. He died on December 2, 1547, at the age of 62. He claimed poverty to the king, but the reality was that he left in Mexico a vast estate and an enormous fortune.

## The Legacy

Hernán Cortés's conquest of Mexico provided the Spanish Empire with the largest addition of land ever obtained by a single person—nine times the size of Spain—as well as the greatest amount of treasure. He earned a reputation for daring, for courage, and also for arrogance and greed.

Had Cortés not discovered Mexico, it seems inevitable that another explorer would have. There were several expeditions to the region prior to his, although these were unsuccessful. His success was due in part to his own skills and in part to simple luck. Had smallpox not devastated the Aztecs, had Spanish ships bringing men and supplies not arrived when they did, his victory would have been far less certain. Initially, Cortés worked hard to build alliances with the Indians he encountered. Their assistance, particularly that of the Tlaxcalans, proved critical to his efforts.

The conquest of Mexico brought about the destruction of the Aztec civilization. Its culture and religion were systematically wiped out by Cortés and those who came after him, determined to build a "New Spain" where they would be lords and rulers. For generations, Indians would suffer in abject poverty while Spaniards built lavish estates and established strict policies regulating trade, ensuring that all goods and raw materials went directly to Spain. Mexico eventually achieved its independence, but to this day much of its Indian population struggles with poverty.

The Catholic Church that Cortés forcefully installed in Mexico continues to thrive. Indeed, Latin America is one of the areas where the modern Catholic Church is experiencing its greatest growth.

In Mexico, Cortés is remembered as a villain. Portraits of him frequently show an ugly, misshapen man, in contrast with most reports of those who knew him. These conflicting portraits reflect the uncertainty about right and wrong when two very different cultures collide.

Cortés was not troubled by this uncertainty. He was to the end a *conquistador*, a man continually searching for new lands to explore and new worlds to conquer.

# CHRONOLOGY

1485     Cortés is born in Medellín, Spain.

1492     Christopher Columbus discovers the New World, inspiring Cortés and others to become explorers. Meanwhile, King Ferdinand and Queen Isabella expell all the Jewish citizens from Spain.

1501     After studying law in Salamanca, Cortés returns to Medellín.

1502     Montezuma becomes ruler of the Aztecs.

## TIMELINE

Cortés is born

Montezuma becomes ruler of the Aztecs

**1492**

**1504**

**1485**

**1502**

Columbus discovers New World

Cortés arrives in Hispaniola

| | |
|---|---|
| 1504 | Cortés lands in Santo Domingo, Hispaniola (now Haiti). |
| 1509 | Illness prevents Cortés from joining expedition to explore the Atlantic coasts of Colombia and Panama. |
| 1511 | Cortés joins expedition to explore Cuba. |
| 1515 | Cortés marries Catalina Juárez due to threats by her brother, Juan. |
| 1517 | First expedition to the Yucatán under the command of Hernández de Córdoba. |
| 1518 | Cortés leaves Santiago on November 18; sails to Trinidad. |
| 1519 | Cortés sets sail for the Yucatán on February 10. Founds first Spanish settlement, Vera Cruz, on June 28. Begins moving inland, to explore Aztec kingdom, on August 16. Reaches Tenochtitlán on November 8. Takes Montezuma captive on November 14. |

Cortés begins exploration of Mexico; takes Montezuma captive

The Aztec army is defeated

**1520**

**1547**

**1519**

**1521**

Cortés dies in Spain

Montezuma is killed

1520    Montezuma is killed on June 30. Cortés and his men flee Tenochtitlán on July 1.

1521    Tenochtitlán is seized by Cortés and his men on August 13; the Aztec army is defeated.

1522    Cortés is appointed captain-general of New Spain.

1528    Cortés travels to Spain to meet with king to ask for the right to continue to govern New Spain. The king refuses to name him governor of Mexico.

1530    Cortés returns to New Spain on July 15; marries Doña Juana de Zuñiga.

1536    Cortés explores Pacific Coast of Mexico; names this territory "California" after a fictional island.

1540    Cortés returns to Spain to ask for support to explore the South Seas; he is denied.

1547    Cortés dies in Spain on December 2.

# GLOSSARY

**ACOLYTE**   assistant to a priest

**ALCALDE**   mayor

**BRAZIERS**   containers used for heating incense

**CABALLERÍA**   a building plot and land to farm

**CACIQUE**   leader of a town or village

**CALIPHATE**   a system of rule based in Islamic tradition; the *caliph*, or leader, is thought to be a successor to the Prophet Muhammad

**ENCOMIENDAS**   the legal right to a number of native workers to provide slave labor

**LANCE**   a long spear used by soldiers mounted on horseback

**LITTER**   an elaborate couch carried on the shoulders of servants

**LOPE LUZIO**   Totonac phrase meaning "prince" or "great lord"

**MATCHLOCK**   a forerunner of the rifle

**PAGE**   an attendant to a member of a noble or royal family; often the first step toward knighthood in medieval society

**PIKE**   sharply pointed spike

**SALT PORK**   similar to bacon but fattier and not cured by smoke

**TLACHTLI**   Aztec sport where players put a rubber ball through two large stone hoops using only their elbows or hips

**YUCCA**   a root vegetable

# BIBLIOGRAPHY

de Gómara, Francisco López. *Cortés: The Life of the Conqueror by his Secretary* (translated and edited by Lesley Byrd Simpson). Berkeley: University of California Press, 1964.

de Madariaga, Salvador. *Hernán Cortés*. Chicago: Henry Regnery Company, 1955.

Díaz, Bernal. *The Conquest of New Spain* (translated by J.M. Cohen). Middlesex, U.K.: Penguin Books, 1963.

Elliott, J.H. *Imperial Spain, 1469-1716*. New York: St. Martin's Press, 1964.

Fuentes, Carlos. *The Buried Mirror: Reflections on Spain and the New World*. New York: Houghton Mifflin, 1992.

Innes, Hammond. *The Conquistadors*. New York: Alfred A. Knopf, 1969.

Kamen, Henry. *Empire: How Spain Became a World Power, 1492–1763*. New York: HarperCollins, 2003.

Levy, Buddy. *Conquistador: Hernán Cortés, King Montezuma, and the Last Stand of the Aztecs*. New York: Bantam Books, 2008.

Mariéjol, Jean Hippolyte. *The Spain of Ferdinand and Isabella*. New Brunswick, N.J.: Rutgers University Press, 1961.

Thomas, Hugh. *Conquest: Montezuma, Cortés, and the Fall of Old Mexico*. New York: Simon & Schuster, 1993.

## WEB SITES

Index of Conquistadors
http://www.pbs.org/conquistadors/cortes/

Medieval Sourcebook: Christopher Columbus
http://www.fordham.edu/halsall/source/Columbus1.html

# FURTHER RESOURCES

Bingham, Jane. *The Aztec Empire*. Chicago: Raintree Books, 2007.

Cortés, Hernán. *Letters from Mexico* (translated by Anthony Pagden). New Haven, Conn.: Yale University Press, 2001.

Crompton, Samuel Willard. *Robert de la Salle*. New York: Chelsea House, 2009.

Koestler-Grack, Rachel A. *Ferdinand Magellan*. New York: Chelsea House, 2009.

Lace, William W. *Captain James Cook*. New York: Chelsea House, 2009.

———. *Sir Francis Drake*. New York: Chelsea House, 2009.

Mann, Charles C. *1491: New Revelations of the Americas Before Columbus*. New York: Vintage Books, 2006.

Townsend, Richard F. *The Aztecs*. New York: Thames & Hudson, 2000.

Worth, Richard. *Vasco da Gama*. New York: Chelsea House, 2009.

## WEB SITES

**Elizabethan Era: Famous Explorers**
http://www.elizabethan-era.org.uk/hernando-cortes.htm
*Biography, timeline, and other interesting facts about Hernán Cortés.*

**European Explorers: Hernán Cortés**
http://www.cdli.ca/CITE/excortes.htm
*Various links to information about Hernán Cortés.*

**Latin American Studies: The Aztecs**
http://www.latinamericanstudies.org/aztecs.htm
*Detailed information about the Aztec Empire, including pictures of artifacts used by the subjects and royalty, diagrams of the Aztec calendar, and links to museum exhibits.*

Minnesota State University, Mankato E-museum

http://www.mnsu.edu/emuseum/prehistory/latinamerica/meso/
cultures/aztec_empire.html

*A virtual museum with online exhibits with content on archaeology, biological anthropology, cultural anthropology, history, and related subjects.*

Modern History Sourcebook: Hernando Cortés

http://www.fordham.edu/halsall/mod/1520cortes.html

*Cortés's second letter to King Charles V in 1520.*

PBS: *The Border*

http://www.pbs.org/kpbs/theborder/history/timeline/1.html

*Online version of the PBS show* The Border, *about the history of the U.S.-Mexico border.*

PBS: *The Conquistadors*

http://www.pbs.org/opb/conquistadors/

*Online educational resource for middle-school and high-school classrooms to learn about Spanish explorers in the New World and the legacy of their contact with Native Americans.*

# PICTURE CREDITS

# INDEX

# ABOUT THE AUTHOR

**HEATHER LEHR WAGNER** is a writer and editor. She is the author of more than 40 books exploring political and social issues for middle-school and high-school readers. She earned a BA in political science from Duke University, and an MA in government from the College of William and Mary.